THOMAS HENRY HUXLEY

From a Photograph by Elliott and Fry

Frontispiece

THOMAS HENRY HUXLEY

A CHARACTER SKETCH

BY

LEONARD HUXLEY

Select Bibliographies Reprint Series

BOOKS FOR LIBRARIES PRESS
FREEPORT, NEW YORK

First Published 1920
Reprinted 1969

574.0924
H98π
114724
July 1980

STANDARD BOOK NUMBER:
8369-5132-8

LIBRARY OF CONGRESS CATALOG CARD NUMBER:
76-102247

PRINTED IN THE UNITED STATES OF AMERICA

CONTENTS

ILLUSTRATIONS

I

INTRODUCTORY

THE object of a full-dress biography is to present as complete a picture as may be of a man and his work, the influence of his character upon his achievement, the struggle with opposing influences to carry out some guiding purpose or great idea. With abundant documents at hand the individual development, the action of events upon character, and of character upon events, can be shown in the spontaneous freedom of letters, as well as in considered publications. But this little book is not a full-dress biography, although it may induce readers to turn to the larger *Life and Letters*, in which (or in the *Aphorisms and Reflections of T. H. Huxley*) facts and quotations can be turned up by means of the index ; it is designed rather as a character sketch, to show not so much the work done as what manner of man Huxley was, and the spirit in which he undertook that work. It will not be a history of his scientific investigations or his philosophical researches ; it will be personal, while from the personal side illustrating his attitude towards his scientific and philosophical thought.

1

EARLY DAYS

THOMAS HENRY HUXLEY was born ten years after Waterloo, while the country was still in the backwash of the long-drawn Napoleonic wars. It was a time of material reconstruction and expansion, while social reconstruction lagged sadly and angrily behind. The year of his birth saw the first railway opened in England ; it was seven years before electoral reform began, with its well-meant but dispiriting sequel in the new Poor Law. The defeat of the political and aggressive cause which had imposed itself upon the revolutionary inspiration of freedom strengthened the old orthodoxies here. Questioning voices were raised at their proper peril.

Thomas Henry was the seventh child of George Huxley and Rachel Withers, his wife. He was born on May 4, 1825, at half-past nine in the morning, according to the entry in the family Bible, at Ealing, where his father was senior assistant-master in the well-known school of Dr. Nicholas, of Wadham College, Oxford. The good doctor, who had succeeded his father-in-law here in 1791, was enough of a public character to have his name parodied by Thackeray as Dr. Tickleus.

"I am not aware," writes Huxley playfully in an autobiographical sketch,

> that any portents preceded my arrival in this world ; but in my childhood I remember hearing a traditional account of the manner in which I lost the chance of an endowment of great practical value.

The windows of my mother's room were open, in consequence of the unusual warmth of the weather. For the same reason, probably, a neighbouring bee-hive had swarmed, and the new colony, pitching on the window-sill, was making its way into the room when the horrified nurse shut down the sash. If that well-meaning woman had only abstained from her ill-timed interference, the swarm might have settled on my lips, and I should have been endowed with that mellifluous eloquence which, in this country, leads far more surely than worth, capacity, or honest work, to the highest places in Church and State. But the opportunity was lost, and I have been obliged to content myself through life with saying what I mean in the plainest of plain language, than which, I suppose, there is no habit more ruinous to a man's prospects of advancement.

The fact that he received the name of the doubting apostle was by no means one of those superhuman coincidences in which some naïve people see portents. In later years my father used to make humorous play with its appropriateness, but in plain fact he was named after his grandfather, Thomas Huxley. I have not traced the origin of the Henry.

Both parents were of dark complexion, and all the children were dark-haired and dark-eyed. The father was tall, and, I believe, well set-up: a miniature shows him with abundant, brown, curling hair brushed high above a good forehead, giving the effect, so fashionable in 1830, of a high-peaked head. The features are well cut and regular; the nose rather long and inclined to be aquiline; the cheeks well covered; the eyes, under somewhat arched brows, expressive and interesting. Outwardly, there is a certain resemblance traceable between the miniature and a daguerrotype of Huxley at nineteen; but the debt, physical and mental, owed to either parent is thus recorded:—

Physically, I am the son of my mother so completely—even down to peculiar movements of the hands, which made their appearance in me as I reached the age she had when I noticed them—that I can hardly find any trace of my father in myself, except an inborn faculty for drawing, which, unfortunately in my case, has never been cultivated; a hot temper, and that amount of tenacity of purpose which unfriendly observers sometimes call obstinacy.

My mother was a slender brunette, of an emotional and energetic temperament, and possessed of the most piercing black eyes I ever saw in a woman's head. With no more education than other women of the middle classes in her day, she had an excellent mental capacity. Her most distinguishing characteristic, however, was rapidity of thought. If one ventured to suggest that she had not taken much time to arrive at any conclusion, she would say: "I cannot help it; things flash across me." That peculiarity has been passed on to me in full strength; it has often stood me in good stead; it has sometimes played me sad tricks, and it has always been a danger. But, after all, if my time were to come over again, there is nothing I would less willingly part with than my inheritance of mother-wit.

Restless, talkative, untiring to the day of her death, she was at sixty-six "as active and energetic as a young woman." To her he was devoted.

As a child my love for her was a passion. I have lain awake for hours crying because I had a morbid fear of her death; her approbation was my greatest reward, her displeasure my greatest punishment.

About his childhood, he writes,

I have next to nothing to say. In after years my mother, looking at me almost reproachfully, would sometimes say, "Ah! you were such a pretty boy!"

whence I had no difficulty in concluding that I had not fulfilled my early promise in the matter of looks. In fact, I have a distinct recollection of certain curls of which I was vain, and of a conviction that I closely resembled that handsome, courtly gentleman, Sir Herbert Oakley, who was vicar of our parish, and who was as a god to us country folk because he was occasionally visited by the then Prince George of Cambridge. I remember turning my pinafore wrong side forwards in order to represent a surplice, and preaching to my mother's maids in the kitchen as nearly as possible in Sir Herbert's manner one Sunday morning, when the rest of the family were at church. That is the earliest indication of the strong clerical affinities which my friend Mr. Herbert Spencer has always ascribed to me, though I fancy they have, for the most part, remained in a latent state.

He was not a precocious child, nor pushed forward by early instruction. His native talent for drawing, had it been cultivated, might have brought him into the front rank of artists; but on the perverse principle, then common, that training is either useless to native capacity or ruins it, he remained untaught, and his vigorous draughtsmanship, invaluable as it was in his scientific career, never reached its full technical perfection. But the sketches which he delighted to make on his travels reveal the artist's eye, if not his trained hand.

His regular schooling was of the scantiest. For two years, from the age of eight to ten, he was at the Ealing school. It was a semi-public school of the old unreformed type. What did a little boy learn there? The rudiments of Latin, of arithmetic, and divinity may be regarded as certain. Greek is improbable, and, in fact, I think my father had no school foundation to build upon when he took up Greek at the age of fifty-five in order to read in the original precisely what Aristotle had written, and not what he was said to have written, about his dissection of the heart.

For the rest, his experience of such a school, before Dr. Arnold's reforming spirit had made itself felt over the country, is eloquent testimony to the need of it.

> Though my way of life [he writes] has made me acquainted with all sorts and conditions of men, from the highest to the lowest, I deliberately affirm that the society I fell into at school was the worst I have ever known. We boys were average lads, with much the same inherent capacity for good and evil as any others; but the people who were set over us cared about as much for our intellectual and moral welfare as if they were baby-farmers. We were left to the operation of the struggle for existence among ourselves; bullying was the least of the ill practices current among us.

One bright spot in these recollections was the licking of an intolerable bully, a certain wild-cat element in him making up for lack of weight. But, alas for justice, " I —the victor—had a black eye, while he—the vanquished —had none, so that I got into disgrace and he did not." A dozen years later he ran across this lad in Sydney, acting as an ostler, a transported convict who had, more-over, undergone more than one colonial conviction.

This brief school career was ended by the break-up of the Ealing establishment. After Dr. Nicholas's death, his sons tried to carry on the school; but the numbers fell off, and George Huxley, about 1835, returned to his native town of Coventry as manager of the Coventry Savings Bank, while his daughters eked out the slender family resources by keeping school.

Meantime, it does not seem that the boy Tom, as he was generally called, received much regular instruction. On the other hand, he learned a great deal for himself. He had an inquiring mind, and a singularly early turn for

metaphysical speculation, He read everything he could
lay hands on in his father's library. We catch a glimpse
of him at twelve, lighting his candle before dawn, and,
with blanket pinned round his shoulders, sitting up in
bed to read Hutton's *Geology*. We see him discussing
all manner of questions with his parents and friends ; and,
indeed, his eager and inquiring mind made it possible for
him to have friends considerably older than himself.
One of these was his brother-in-law, Dr. Cooke of
Coventry, who married his sister Ellen in 1839.
Through Dr. Cooke he became, as a boy, interested in
human anatomy, with results that deeply affected his
career for good and for evil.

The extraordinary attraction [he writes] I felt
towards the intricacies of living structure proved
nearly fatal to me at the outset. I was a mere boy
—I think between thirteen and fourteen years of
age—when I was taken by some older student
friends of mine to the first *post-mortem* examination
I ever attended. All my life I have been most
unfortunately sensitive to the disagreeables which
attend anatomical pursuits, but on this occasion my
curiosity overpowered all other feelings, and I spent
two or three hours in gratifying it. I did not cut
myself, and none of the ordinary symptoms of
dissection-poison supervened; but poisoned I was
somehow, and I remember sinking into a strange
state of apathy. By way of a last chance, I was
sent to the care of some good, kind people, friends
of my father's, who lived in a farmhouse in the
heart of Warwickshire. I remember staggering
from my bed to the window, on the bright spring
morning after my arrival, and throwing open the
casement. Life seemed to come back on the wings
of the breeze, and to this day the faint odour of
wood-smoke, like that which floated across the farm-
yard in the early morning, is as good to me as the
"sweet south upon a bed of violets." I soon

recovered; but for years I suffered from occasional paroxysms of internal pain, and from that time my constant friend, hypochondriacal dyspepsia, commenced his half-century of co-tenancy of my fleshly tabernacle.

In this life-long recurrence of suffering he was like his great friend and leader, Darwin. Each worked to his utmost under a severe handicap, which, it must be remembered, in Darwin's case, was by far the more constant and more disabling, though, happily, an ample fortune absolved him from the troubles of pecuniary stress.

Years afterwards, one of these " good, kind friends " calls up the picture of " Tom Huxley looking so thin and ill, and pretending to make hay with one hand, while in the other he held a German book."

How did he come thus early to teach himself German, a study which was to have undreamed-of consequences in his future ? He learned it so well that, while still a young man, he could read it—rare faculty—almost as swiftly as English ; and he was one of the swiftest readers I have known. Thus equipped, he had the advantage of being one of the few English men of science who made it a practice to follow German research at first hand, and turn its light upon their own work.

The learning of German was one half of the debt he owed to Carlyle, the other being an intense hatred of shams of every sort and kind. He had begun to read the fiery-tongued prophet in his earliest teens, and caught his inspiration at once. *Sartor Resartus* was for many years his Enchiridion (he says), while the translations from the German, the references to German literature and philosophy, fired him to read the originals.

As to other languages, his testimonials in 1842 record that he reads French with facility, and has a fair knowledge of Latin. Thus he took the *Suites à Buffon* with him on the *Rattlesnake* as a reference book in zoology. As to Latin, he was not content with a knowledge of its use in natural science. Beyond the minimum knowledge needful to interpret, or to confer, the "barbarous binomials" of scientific nomenclature, he was led on to read early scientific works published in Latin; and in philosophy, something of Spinoza; and later, massive tomes of the Fathers, whether to barb his exquisite irony in dissecting St. George Mivart's exposition of the orthodox Catholic view of Evolution, or in the course of his studies in Biblical criticism. Of Greek, mention has already been made. He employed his late beginnings of the language not only to follow Aristotle's work as an anatomist, but to aid his studies in Greek philosophy and New Testament criticism, and to enjoy Homer in the original. In middle life, too, he dipped sufficiently into Norwegian and Danish to grapple with some original scientific papers. When he was fifteen, Italian as well as German is set down by him in his list of things to be learnt, though for some time the pressure of preparing for the London matriculation barred the way; and on the voyage of the *Rattlesnake* he spent many hours making out Dante with the aid of a dictionary. No doubt, also, he must have read some Italian poetry with his wife during their engagement and early married days, for she had a fair acquaintance with Italian, as well as equalling his knowledge of German. When he was past sixty and ill-health, cutting short his old activities, had sent him to seek rest and change in Italy, he took up Italian again, and plunged into the authorities on the very interesting prehistoric archæology of Italy.

To return to his early development. There is extant a fragmentary little journal of his, begun when he was fifteen, and kept irregularly for a couple of years. Here

B

the early bent of his mind is clearly revealed; it pre-figures the leading characteristics of his mature intellect. He jots down any striking thought or saying he comes across in the course of his reading; he makes practical experiments to test his theories; above all, his insatiable curiosity to find out the "why" and "how" of things makes him speculate on their causes, and discuss with his friends the right and wrong of existing institutions.

This curiosity to make out how things work is common to most healthy boys; to probe deep into the reasoned "why" is rare. It makes the practical mechanic into the man of science. Possessing both these qualities as he did, it is easy to understand his own description of his early ambitions:—

> As I grew older, my great desire was to be a mechanical engineer, but the fates were against this; and, while very young, I commenced the study of medicine under a medical brother-in-law. But, though the Institute of Mechanical Engineers would certainly not own me, I am not sure that I have not all along been a sort of mechanical engineer *in partibus infidelium.* I am now occasion-ally horrified to think how little I ever knew or cared about medicine as the art of healing. The only part of my professional course which really and deeply interested me was physiology, which is the mechanical engineering of living machines; and, notwithstanding that natural science has been my proper business, I am afraid there is very little of the genuine naturalist in me. I never collected anything, and species work was always a burden to me; what I cared for was the architectural and engineering part of the business, the working out the wonderful unity of plan in the thousands and thousands of diverse living constructions, and the modifications of similar apparatuses to serve diverse ends.

One or two typical extracts may be given from the *Journal*, which opens with a quotation from Novalis : "Philosophy can bake no bread ; but it can prove for us God, freedom, and immortality. Which, now, is more practical, Philosophy or Economy?" Later comes a quotation from Lessing, which involved a cardinal principle that he claimed for himself, and demanded of his pupils : accept no authority without verifying it for yourself :—

> I hate all people who want to found sects. It is not error, but sects—it is not error, but sectarian error, nay, and even sectarian truth, which causes the unhappiness of mankind.

Electricity interests him specially ; among other experiments, while theorizing upon them, he makes a galvanic battery "in view of experiment to get crystallized carbon : got it deposited, but not crystallized."

He is a young Radical in his opposition to anything like injustice, though frankly admitting that youth is not infallible. One of his boyish speculations was as to what would become of things if their qualities were taken away. While on this quest, he got hold of Sir William Hamilton's *Logic*, and read it to such good effect that when, years afterwards, he sat down to the greater philosophers, he found that he already had a clear notion of where the key of metaphysics lay. The following extract from the *Journal* shows that he already had a characteristic point of view :—

> Had a long talk with my mother and father about the right to make Dissenters pay church rates, and whether there ought to be any Establishment. I maintain that there ought not in both cases—I wonder what will be my opinion ten years hence ? I think now that it is against all laws of justice to force men to support a church with whose opinions they cannot conscientiously agree. The argument

that the rate is so small is very fallacious. It is as much a sacrifice of principle to do a little wrong as to do a great one.

His friend, George Anderson May, with whom the boy of fifteen has "a long argument on the nature of the soul and the difference between it and matter," was then a man of six and twenty, in business at Hinckley.

> I maintained that it could not be proved that matter is *essentially*, as to its base, different from soul. Mr. M. wittily said soul was the perspiration of matter.

> We cannot find the absolute basis of matter; we only know it by its properties; neither know we the soul in any other way. *Cogito ergo sum* is the only thing that we *certainly* know.

> Why may not soul and matter be of the same substance (*i.e.*, basis whereon to fix qualities; for we cannot suppose a quality to exist *per se*, it must have a something to qualify), but with different qualities?

Hamilton's analysis of the Absolute, once learned, was never forgotten. It was a philosophic touchstone, understood by the boy, applied by the man. With the Absolute, an entity stripped of perceptible qualities, an "hypostatized negation," he could have no traffic. The Cartesian motto of thought as the essence of existence became another fixed point for him, and his last questioning phrase half suggests the line of reasoning which, as he afterwards put it, asserts that, philosophically speaking, materialism is but spiritualism turned inside out.

III

MEDICAL TRAINING

At fifteen and a-half he began his medical training. Engineering, it seems, was not within his parents' purview; the boy was thoughtful and scientific; medicine was then the only avenue for science, and medicine loomed large on their horizon, for two of their daughters had married doctors. Of these, Dr. Cooke had already begun to give him instruction in anatomy; it looked as though destiny had marked out his career.

In those days, the future doctor began by being apprenticed to a regular practitioner; he picked up a great deal from compounding medicines, watching out-patients in the surgery, and attending simple cases, especially if he had a capable man to work under. At the same time he prepared for his future examinations, and got ready to walk the hospitals.

This apprenticeship was a strongly formative period in Huxley's life. He was bound to Dr. Chandler, of Rotherhithe, and joined him in this quarter of poverty and struggle on January 7, 1841. The little journal shows him busy with all the subjects of the London Matriculation: History ancient and modern, Greek, Latin, English Grammar, Chemistry, Mathematics, Physics, with German also and Physiology, besides experimental work in natural science, philosophical analysis, and a copious course of Carlyle.

But this book-work was the least of the influences acting upon him. Dr. Chandler had charge of the parish doctoring, and the boy's experiences among the

poor in the dock region of the East End left an efface-
able mark.   It was a grim, living commentary on his
Carlyle.   For the rest of his life the cause of the poor
appealed vividly to him, because he had at least seen
something of the way in which the poor lived.   People
who were suffering from nothing but slow starvation
would come to him for medical aid.   One scene above all
was burnt into his memory: a sick girl in a wretched
garret, the boy visitor saying as gently as he could that
her sole need was better food, and the sister of the
starved child who turned upon him with a kind of
choking passion, and, pulling from her pocket a few pence
and half-pence and holding them out, cried: " That is all
I get for six-and-thirty hours' work, and you talk about
giving her proper food."

When, after a full year, he left Rotherhithe for the
north of London, to be apprenticed—as his elder brother,
James, had already been apprenticed—to his other
medical brother-in-law, Dr. Scott, he saw more of this
teeming, squalid life in the filthy courts and alleys
through which he used to pass on his way to the library
of the College of Surgeons.

What, in later life, he tried to do to better this state
of things was not the usual philanthropic work, but the
endeavour to bring intellectual light to the ignorant
toilers, to strip away make-believe, and provide some
machinery by which to catch and utilize capacity.

Great was the change from the surroundings of
Rotherhithe to the home atmosphere of the Scotts.   He
was now with his favourite sister Eliza, his senior by
twelve years, who was a second mother to him.   Her
sympathy and encouragement did much for him; her
belief in the future of " her boy " was redoubled upon his
first public success when, at the age of seventeen, he won
the second prize, the silver medal of the Apothecaries'

Company, in a competitive examination in botany.
" For a young hand," he tells us, " I worked really hard
from eight or nine in the morning until twelve at night,
besides a long, hot summer's walk over to Chelsea, two
or three times a week, to hear Lindley. A great part of
the time—*i.e.*, June and July—I worked till sunrise.
The result was a sort of ophthalmia, which kept me from
reading at night for months afterwards."

The lively and amusing description of the examination
and its sequel is given in full in the *Life ;* suffice it to
say that when four o'clock came and only two com-
petitors were left writing hard, and not half through the
paper, they were allowed to go on by general consent.
By eight o'clock the seventeen-year-old came to an end ;
the older man went on until nine. This was John
Ellerton Stocks, afterwards M.D. and a distinguished
traveller and botanist in India. To him fell the first
prize ; the boy, to his own astonishment and the wild
delight of his sister, won the second.

In October, 1842, a couple of months after this
success, both he and his brother James entered Charing
Cross Hospital as free scholars. Here he worked very
hard—when it pleased him—took up all sorts of pursuits
and dropped them again, and read everything he could
lay hands upon, including novels. The one instructor by
whom he was really impressed, and for whom he did his
utmost, was Wharton Jones, lecturer on physiology.
" He was extremely kind and helpful to the youngster,
who, I am afraid, took up more of his time than he had
any right to do." Wharton Jones assuredly was one of
those born teachers who love to give time and all to a
keen and promising pupil. It is good to know that the
bread he cast upon the waters returned to him after
many days. Wharton Jones, too, was responsible for the
publication of the young man's first scientific paper, in

the *Medical Gazette* of 1845. Investigating things for himself, the student of nineteen had found a hitherto undiscovered membrane in the root of the human hair, which received the name of Huxley's layer.

No doubt his work was, as he confesses, not systematically spread over his various subjects; and his energy was fitful, though it was energy that struck his contemporaries, who gave the name of the " Sign of the Head and Microscope " to the familiar silhouette of him as he sat before a window poring over his dissections, while they swarmed out into the quadrangle after lectures.

He achieved brilliant successes as a student. In 1843 he won the first prize in Chemistry, with a note that his " extraordinary diligence and success in the pursuit of this branch of science do him infinite honour," as well as the first prize in Anatomy and Physiology. He was only twenty when, in 1845, he went up for his M.B. at London University, and won a gold medal in his favourite subjects of Anatomy and Physiology, being second in that section.

Early in 1846, being still too young to qualify at the College of Surgeons, yet confronted by the imperative necessity for earning his own bread, he applied, at the suggestion of his fellow-student, Lyon Playfair, for service as a naval surgeon, passed the necessary examination, and went to Haslar. His official chief, old John Richardson, of Arctic fame, silently kept an eye upon him, and, failing to get him one of the coveted resident appointments, kept him, all unaware and ill-content, at Haslar till something worthy of his scientific abilities should turn up. Seven months passed ; then came the chance of sailing on the surveying and exploring ship *Rattlesnake*, under Captain Owen Stanley, R.N., brother of the more famous Dean, who was in want of an assistant-surgeon with a turn for science.

IV

THE VOYAGE OF THE *RATTLESNAKE*, AND ITS SEQUEL

THE three friends, Darwin, Hooker, and Huxley, were alike in this, that each in his turn began his career with a great voyage of scientific discovery in one of H.M. ships. Darwin was twenty-two when the *Beagle* sailed for the Straits of Magellan; Hooker, also, was twenty-two when he sailed for the Antarctic with Ross on the *Erebus*; Huxley was but twenty-one when he set forth with Owen Stanley for Australian waters to survey the Great Barrier Reef and New Guinea. Each found in the years of distant travel a withdrawal from the distracting bustle of ordinary life, which enabled him to concentrate upon original work and to reflect deeply, unhampered by current doctrines; each came back, not only deeply impressed by the elemental problems of life, but "salted" with the sea and the discipline of the sea.

> It was good to live under sharp discipline; to be down on the realities of existence by living on bare necessaries; to find how extremely well worth living life seemed to be when one woke up from a night's rest on a soft plank, with the sky for canopy, and cocoa and weevily biscuit the sole prospect for breakfast; and, more especially, to learn to work for the sake of what I got for myself out of it, even if it all went to the bottom and I along with it.

Huxley was not so well situated as either Darwin, the well-to-do amateur who was naturalist to the expedition, or Hooker, the son of a distinguished botanist, receiving

17

many privileges from his father's friend, Captain Ross, while officially he was but an assistant-surgeon and second naturalist. Huxley had neither friends nor influence beyond the simple recommendation of "old John" Richardson. Macgillivray, the naturalist, and the Captain himself had scientific interests, but not so the other officers, who disliked seeing the decks messed by the contents of the tow-net. Yet they were "as good fellows as sailors ought to be, and generally are," though they did not understand why he should be so zealous in pursuit of the objects which his friends the middies christened "Buffons," after his volume of the *Suites à Buffon*. As assistant-surgeon he messed with the middies, but his good spirits and fun and freedom from any assumption of superiority made the boys his good comrades.

From the first he was very busy, glorying in the prospect of being able to give himself up to his favourite pursuits, without thereby neglecting the proper duties of life. A twenty-eight gun frigate was anything but a floating palace. The *Rattlesnake* was badly fitted out, and always leaky ; the lower deck gave a head-space of four feet ten, which was cramping to a man of five feet eleven ; but he had the run of the commodious chart-room, as arranged for a surveying ship, and would have had the run of the library if Captain Stanley's requisition for books had not been "overlooked" by a parsimonious Admiralty. His tiny cabin was light enough to work in on a dull day ; but as for the possibility of making a scientific collection, it was but seven feet by six, by five feet six inches high, and infested with cockroaches to boot.

His work took shape in a mass of drawings and descriptions from the dissection of the perishable marine organisms of the tropical seas, and, yet more important, in the new classification he established upon anatomical grounds. His first papers were sent to the Linnean Society by Captain Stanley; the later and more important he sent himself to Edward Forbes, the most interested and helpful of the biologists to whom he had been introduced before he left England. To his angry disappointment, no news of them, no acknowledgment even, reached him on the other side of the world; it was not till he returned, after the four years of his voyage, that he found they had been published by the Royal Society, and had established his reputation as a first-rate investigator. But, though with much difficulty the scientific authorities enabled him to secure the promised Government grant for his book, and a temporary billet ashore while he worked at it, he was only able to publish his *Oceanic Hydrozoa;* a vast quantity of his researches remained unpublished, and subsequent investigators, going over the same ground, won the credit for them.

The other scientific interest strongly aroused on the voyage was anthropology. The cruise of the *Rattlesnake* provided one of the last opportunities of visiting tribes who had never before seen a white man. The young surgeon made a point of getting into touch with these primitive people at Cape York, and in the islands off New Guinea. He made a preliminary exploration through the uncharted bush of Queensland with the ill-fated Kennedy, and all but accompanied him on his disastrous journey to Cape York, when of all the party only two were rescued, through the devotion of the faithful native guide. He exchanged names, and therefore affinities, with a friendly native of the Louisiades, and learned much at first hand as to their physical and mental characteristics, which stimulated his subsequent anthropological work.

The Australian voyage, then, provided a magnificent

field for original research and original thought: the unknown naval surgeon returned from it to find himself recognized as one of the coming men. Contact with the larger world had broadened his outlook; the touch of naval discipline concentrated his powers. But Australia gave him another gift. He met at Sydney his future wife. The young couple fell in love almost at first sight, and became engaged. They were of the same age, 22; they hoped to get married when he was promoted to the rank of full surgeon; they were destined to wait seven-and-a-half years before she returned home to fulfil his early jesting prophecy of making her a Frau Professorin. Here, again, was stern disciplining on the part of destiny. For the first years they were able to meet during the intervals between the long surveying cruises of the ship; they cheated the months of separation by keeping journals for each other. But for nearly five years they were parted by twelve thousand miles of sea, and, worse, by slow sailing ships, when letters would take five months or more to receive an answer, which by that time might be entirely at cross purposes with the changed aspect of affairs. The possibilities of estrangement were incalculable. Their lives were developing on entirely different lines. He had been admitted to the inmost circle of men of science as an intellectual peer; he was elected F.R.S. when he was barely twenty-six, and received the Royal Medal the following year, as well as being chosen to serve on the Council of the Society; he wrote; he lectured at the Royal Institution. And yet, with all the support of the leaders in science, he could not find any post wherein to earn his bread and butter. He stood for professorships at Toronto, at Sydney, at Aberdeen, Cork and King's College, London. The Admiralty, in March, 1854, even refused further leave for the publication of the scientific work to do which he had been sent out. He

From a Daguerrotype made in 1846

To face p. 20

took the bull by the horns, and, rather than return to the hopeless routine of a naval surgeon, let the Admiralty fulfil their threat to deprive him of his appointment, and the slender pay which was his only certain support. His scientific friends besought him to hold on; something must come in his way, and a brilliant career was before him; but was he justified, he asked himself again and again, in pursuing the glorious phantom, so miserably paid at the best, instead of taking up some business career, perhaps in Australia, and ending the cruel delay which bore so hardly upon the woman he loved? Yet would not this be a desertion of his manifest duty, his intellectual duty to himself and to Science? He knew full well that there was only one course which could bring him either hope or peace, and yet, between the two calls upon him, he never knew which course he would ultimately follow.

For her there was no such mental development. Assuredly she kept up her literary pursuits, her study of German, in which they had found common ground of interest, for she had spent two years at school in Germany; but she was cribbed and cabined by the ups and downs of early colonial life, and the fluctuating ventures upon which her father delighted to embark; there was, naturally, no possibility of her moving in the stimulating intellectual society which was his, and hope deferred wore upon her as the laurels of scientific success were consistently followed by failure in all solid prospects. Yet neither possible misunderstandings, nor actual disappointments, had power to shake the foundations of their mutual trust, and the inspiration of the ideal which each built on the other's so different character; the one more compact of fire, the other more of noble patience, different, but alike in a largeness of soul and freedom from pettiness, which made their forty years of united life something out of the common. She believed in him; in the darkest season of disappointment she bade him remember that a man should pursue those things for which he is most fitted, let them be what they will. Her "noble and self-sacrificing" words brought him comfort, and banished "the spectre of a wasted life that had passed before him—a vision of that servant who hid his talent in a napkin and buried it."

At last the gleams of promise, which had begun to gather, broke through the clouds. On the sudden death of Professor Jamieson, his good friend Edward Forbes was called away in the spring of 1854 to take the Edinburgh professorship. At a few days' notice Huxley was lecturing as Forbes's substitute at the Royal School of Mines. In July he was appointed permanently, with a salary for his course of £100 a year. A few days later his income was doubled. Forbes had held two lecture-ships; the man who had accepted the other drew back, and it was given to Huxley. In August he was "entrusted with the Coast Survey Investigations under the Geological Survey," becoming the regular Naturalist to the Survey the following year, with pay of £200, afterwards increased to £400, rising to £600. The way was clear; the Heathorn family had already determined to come home. Miss Heathorn hâd been very ill; she was still far from strong, and, indeed, one gloomy doctor only gave her six months to live. The lover defied him: "I shall marry her all the same;" but the gloomy doctor was alone in his opinion, and, indeed, she lived till she was nearly eighty-nine. The marriage, which was to bring so much active happiness in a life of much struggle and stress, was celebrated on July 1, 1855. They had become engaged at twenty-two; they had waited and striven—for eight years; they were rewarded by forty years of mutual love and support.

V

LEHRJAHRE

THE award of the Royal Medal was felt by Huxley to be
a turning-point. It was something which convinced the
" practical " people who used to scoff at his " dreamy "
notions, and brought them to urge him on a more
"dreamy" course than ever he dreamed of. "However,"
he remarks, " I take very much my own course now,
even as I have done before—Huxley all over." Without
being blinded by any vanity, he saw in the award and
the general estimate in which it was held a finger-post
showing as clearly as anything can what was the true
career lying open before him. Ambitious in the current
sense of worldly success he was not. The praise of men
stirred a haunting mistrust of their judgment and his own
worthiness. Honours he valued as evidences of power ;
but no more. What possessed him was, as he confessed
in a letter meant only for the eye of his future wife, " an
enormous longing after the highest and best in all shapes
—a longing which haunts me and is the demon which
ever impels me to work, and will let me have no rest
unless I am doing his behests." With the sense of
power stirring within him, he refused to be beholden to
any man. Patronage he abhorred in an age of patronage.
He was ready to accept a helping hand from any one
who thought him capable of forwarding the great cause
in ever so small a way ; but on no other terms. If the
time had come to speak out on any matter, he was

23

resolved to let no merely personal influence restrain him.
He cared only for the praise or blame of the understanding few.   Whatever the popular judgment, he knew
there was a work to be done and that he had power to
do it ; and this was his personal ambition—to do that
work in the world, and to do it without cant and humbug
and self-seeking.   Such were the aims that, newly
returned to England, he confides to the sister who had
ever prophesied great things of " her boy " ; and in the
end he made good the works spoken so boldly, yet surely
in no mere spirit of boasting,   He " left his mark somewhere, clear and distinct," without taint of the insinceri-
ties which he had an almost morbid dread of discovering
in any act of his own.

It was not every one who could dare to range so far
and wide as Huxley did from the original line of investigation he had taken up.   Friends warned him against
what appeared to be a scattering of his energies.   If he
devoted himself to that morphology of the Invertebrates
in which his new and illuminating conceptions had
promptly earned the Royal Medal, he would easily be
the first in his field.   But what he did was in great part
of set purpose.   He was no mere collector of specimens,
no mere describer of species.   He sought the living
processes which determined natural groups ; the theories
he formed needed verification in various directions.
These excursions from the primary line of research were
of great value in broadening the basis of his knowledge.
He also deliberately set aside the years 1854–60 as
a period in which to make himself master of the branches
of science cognate to his own, so that he should be ready
for any special pursuits in any of them.   For he did not
know what was to be his task after the work that had
fallen to him, not of his own choice, at the School of
Mines.   He was to ground himself in each department

by monographic work, and by 1860 might fairly look
forward to fifteen or twenty years of "Meisterjahre,"
when, with the comprehensive views arising from such
training, it should be possible to give a new and healthier
direction to all biological science.   Meanwhile, opportunities must be seized at the risk of a reputation for
desultoriness.

But the irony of circumstances diverted much of his
energy into yet more diverse fields.   When Sir Henry
de la Bèche first offered him the posts of Palæontologist
and Lecturer on Natural History vacated by Professor
Forbes, he says:—

> I refused the former point blank, and accepted
> the latter only provisionally, telling Sir Henry that
> I did not care for fossils, and that I should give up
> Natural History as soon as I could get a physio-
> logical post.   But I held the office for thirty-one
> years, and a large part of my work has been
> palæontological.

Palæontology was his business, and he became
a Master in it also, with the result that he forged
himself a mighty weapon for use in the struggle over
the Origin of Species.

In one of his later Essays he compares the study of
human physiology to the Atlantic Ocean:—

> Like the Atlantic between the Old and the New
> Worlds, its waves wash the shores of the two worlds
> of matter and of mind; its tributary streams flow
> from both; through its waters, as yet unfurrowed
> by the keel of any Columbus, lies the road, if such
> there be, from the one to the other; far away from
> that North-West Passage of mere speculation in
> which so many brave souls have been helplessly
> frozen up.

Such was the spirit in which, after his long day's work,
he added to his labours in physical science a search in

c

another, and to his notion a cognate province of thought and speculation. Many a sleepless night in these years the candle was lighted beside his bed, and for a couple of hours after midnight he would devour works on philosophy—English, German, and French, and occasionally Latin. To a mind at once constructive and intensely critical of unsound construction he added a quality possessed by few professed philosophers—a large knowledge of the workings of life, of the human thinking machine, in addition to various other branches of physical science. As he put it, the laboratory is the forecourt to the temple of philosophy. For the method of the laboratory is but the strict application of the one sound and fruitful mode of reasoning—the method of verification by experiment. Evidence must be tested before being trusted. The first duty of such a method is to question in order to find good reason; Goethe's " tätige Skepsis," a scepticism or questioning which seeks to overcome itself by finding good standing-ground beyond. Authority as such is nothing till verified anew. The creeds of ancient sages, the dogmas of more modern date, must equally bear the light of widening knowledge and the tests that prove the gold or clay of their foundations, the stability of the successive steps by which they proceed.

In all this reading Huxley found nothing to shake what he had learnt long before from Hamilton—the limits set to human knowledge and the impossibility of attaining to the ultimate reality behind the phenomena presented to our cognition. The problems of philosophy, set forth with unsurpassed clearness for all who will read in our great English writers, were not solved by soaring into intellectual mists. To those who declared they had attained this ultimate knowledge by their own inner light or through an alleged revelation in historical

experience, the question remained to be put: How do
you verify your assertion? Is the historical evidence
on which you build trustworthy? And if in certain
departments this evidence is clearly untenable, what
guarantee have you that in other departments evidence
of similar character is tenable? The fine-spun abstrac-
tions of the Platonists and their kin, unchecked by
a natural science which had not yet the appliances
necessary for its growth; the orthodoxies of the various
churches, so singularly differentiated in the course of
development from the simplicity of their nominal
founder—these were based upon assumptions for which
the seeker after reasoned evidence could find no valid
support. Ten years before he coined the word "Agnostic"
to label his attitude towards the unproved, whether
likely or unlikely, in contradistinction to the Gnostics, who
professed to "know" from within apart from external
proof, Huxley described the Agnostic position he had
already reached—the position of suspending judgment
where actual proof is not possible; the attitude of mind
which regards the words "I believe" as a momentous
assertion, not to be uttered on incomplete grounds.
Writing to Charles Kingsley in 1860, he says:—

> I neither deny nor affirm the immortality of man.
> I see no reason for believing in it; but, on the other
> hand, I have no means of disproving it.
>   Pray understand that I have no à priori objections
> to the doctrine. No man who has to deal daily and
> hourly with nature can trouble himself about à priori
> difficulties. Give me such evidence as would justify
> me in believing anything else, and I will believe that.
> Why should I not? It is not half so wonderful as
> the conservation of force, or the indestructibility of
> matter. Whoso clearly appreciates all that is
> implied in the falling of a stone can have no
> difficulty about any doctrine simply on account of

its marvellousness.   But the longer I live the more
obvious it is to me that the most, sacred act of a
man's life is to say and to feel, "I believe such and
such to be true."   All the greatest rewards, and all
the heaviest penalties of existence, cling about that
act.   The universe is one and the same throughout;
and if the condition of my success in unravelling
some little difficulty of anatomy or physiology is
that I shall rigorously refuse to put faith in that
which does not rest on sufficient evidence, I cannot
believe that the great mysteries of existence will be
laid open to me on other terms.   It is of no use to
talk to me of analogies and probabilities.   I know
what I mean when I say I believe in the law of the
inverse square, and I will not rest my life and my
hopes upon weaker convictions. I dare not if I would.

From such a point of view intellectual veracity takes
on a moral aspect; indeed, it is ¸a pillar of morality.
Disregard of it has led to incalculable social wrong and
individual suffering, oppressions and persecutions, unpro-
gressive obscurantism, joined with perverted ideals and
intellectual arrest.   "Ecrasez l'infâme," cried the
reforming Voltaire; his "infamous" was very much
this perverting influence, exaggerated and armed with
power, which had made the great organization of the
Roman Church in his time a monstrous instrument of
autocratic tradition, cruel, rapacious, blindly intolerant,
jealous of light and liberty.   In England the growth of
political liberty had deprived the darkest lights of the
Church of almost all power for active interference in the
administration of the State, though the pressure of
traditionalism exercised itself less crudely, if scarce less
surely, in the Universities, the Press, religious opinion,
and the army of conventional respectability.   So strong
was it in social influence that a man, openly professing
to make a guide of his reason instead of his parson, was
liable to be pushed outside the pale.

VI

VERACITY AND AGNOSTICISM

ONE of the most ticklish of all subjects to handle at this period was the position of the human species in zoological classification. "It was a burning question in the sense that those who touched it were almost certain to burn their fingers severely." In the fifties Sir William Lawrence had been well-nigh ostracized for his book *On Man*, "which now might be read in a Sunday-school without surprising anybody." When Huxley submitted the proofs of *Man's Place in Nature* to "a competent anatomist, and good friend of his," asking him, if he could, to point out any errors of fact, the friend—it was Lawrence himself—declared he could find none, but gave an earnest warning as to the consequences of publication. Here was one of the cases where Huxley's firm resolution applied—to speak out if necessary, regardless of consequences; indeed, he felt sure that all the evil things prophesied would not be so painful to him as the giving up that which he had resolved to do upon grounds which he conceived to be right. As he wrote later (in 1876) :—

> It seemed to me that a man of science has no *raison d'être* at all unless he is willing to face much greater risks than these for the sake of that which he believes to be true ; and further, that to a man of science such risks do not count for much—they are by no means so serious as they are to a man of letters, for example.

29

The book was published, and the friend's forecast was amply justified.

The Boreas of criticism blew his hardest blasts of misrepresentation and ridicule for some years, and I was even, as one of the wicked. Indeed, it surprises me at times to think how any one who had sunk so low could since have emerged into, at any rate, relative respectability. Personally, like the non-corvine personages in the Ingoldsby legend, I did not feel "one penny the worse." Translated into several languages, the book reached a wider public than I had ever hoped for; being largely helped, I imagine, by the Ernulphine advertisements to which I referred. It has had the honour of being freely utilized without acknowledgment by writers of repute; and, finally, it achieved the fate, which is the euthanasia of a scientific work, of being enclosed among the rubble of the foundations of later knowledge, and forgotten.

To my observation, human nature has not sensibly changed during the last thirty years. I doubt not that there are truths as plainly obvious, and as generally denied, as those contained in *Man's Place in Nature*, now awaiting enunciation. If there is a young man of the present generation who has taken as much trouble as I did to assure himself that they are truths, let him come out with them, without troubling his head about the barking of the dogs of St. Ernulphus. *Veritas praevalebit*—some day; and even if she does not prevail in his time, he himself will be all the better and wiser for having tried to help her. And let him recollect that such great reward is full payment for all his labour and pains.

To speak out thus was one side of his passion for veracity. When it was a matter of demonstrable truth, he refused to be intimidated by great names. Already, in his Croonian lecture of 1858, " On the Theory of the Vertebrate Skull," he had challenged, and by direct

morphological investigation overthrown, the theory of
Oken, adopted and enlarged upon by Owen, that the
adult skull is a modified vertebral column. Again, the
great name of Owen, that jealous king of the anatomical
world, had in 1857 supported the assertion, so contrary to
the investigations of Huxley himself and of other
anatomists, that certain anatomical features of the brain
are peculiar to the genus *Homo*, and are a ground for
placing that genus separately from all other mammals—
in a division, Archencephala, apart from and superior to
the rest. Huxley thereupon re-investigated the whole
question, and soon satisfied himself that these structures
were not peculiar to man, but are common to all the
higher and many of the lower apes. This led him to
study the whole question of the structural relations of
man to the next lower existing forms. Without embark-
ing on controversy, he embodied his conclusions in his
teaching.

Thus, in 1860, he was well prepared to follow up
Darwin's words in the *Origin of Species*, " Light will be
thrown on the origin of man and his history," and to
furnish proofs in the field of Development and Vertebrate
Anatomy, which were not among Darwin's many
specialities.

When Owen, at the Oxford meeting of the British
Association, repeated his former assertions, he publicly
took up the challenge. On the technical side, a series of
dissections undertaken by himself, Rolleston, and Flower
displayed the structures for all to see ; on the popular
side, Huxley delivered in 1860 a course of public lectures
which were the basis of his book, *Man's Place in Nature*,
above mentioned.

Here the principle is actively exemplified : speak out
fearlessly at the right moment to strike down that which
is demonstrably false. It is the counterpart to the other

aspect of veracity which will not say "I believe " to an unverified assertion.   These two aspects of the same principle, as has been seen, developed hand in hand in his early career ; but it was the active challenge to ill-based authority which by its courage, not to say audacity, first attracted public notice and public abuse. The other, the apparently negative aspect, came into general notice only after 1869.   Its very reserves, how-ever, resting on a statement of reasons for finding the testimony to certain doctrines insufficient, had long provoked assaults from the upholders of these doctrines, which made no less call upon his courage and endurance. As a philosophic position, however, it was not formally and publicly defined until, in the debates of the Meta-physical Society founded in that year, he invented for himself the label of Agnostic.   The Society was composed of distinguished men, representing almost every shade of opinion and intellectual occupation ;   University pro-fessors, statesmen, lawyers, bishops and deans, a Cardinal, a poet ; men of science and men of letters ; Anglicans, Roman Catholics, Unitarians, Positivists, Freethinkers.

The story is told in his article on " Agnosticism," written in 1889 (*Collected Essays*, v, 237).   After describing how it came about that his mind " steadily gravitated towards the conclusions of Hume and Kant," so well stated by the latter as follows :—

> The greatest and perhaps the sole use of all philosophy of pure reason is, after all, merely negative, since it serves not as an organon for the enlargement (of knowledge), but as a discipline for its delimitation ; and, instead of discovering truth, has only the modest merit of preventing error—

he proceeds :—

When I reached intellectual maturity and began

to ask myself whether I was an atheist, a theist, or a pantheist; a materialist or an idealist; a Christian or a freethinker; I found that the more I learned and reflected the less ready was the answer, until, at last, I came to the conclusion that I had neither art nor part with any of these denominations except the last. The one thing in which most of these good people were agreed was the one thing in which I differed from them. They were quite sure they had attained a certain "gnosis" —had, more or less successfully, solved the problem of existence; while I was quite sure I had not, and had a pretty strong conviction that the problem was insoluble. And, with Hume and Kant on my side, I could not think myself presumptuous in holding fast by that opinion..........

This was my situation when I had the good fortune to find a place among the members of that remarkable confraternity of antagonists, long since deceased, but of green and pious memory, the Metaphysical Society. Every variety of philosophical and theological opinion was represented there, and expressed itself with entire openness; most of my colleagues were -ists of one sort or another; and, however kind and friendly they might be, I, the man without a rag of a label to cover himself with, could not fail to have some of the uneasy feelings which must have beset the historical fox when, after leaving the trap in which his tail remained, he presented himself to his normally elongated companions. So I took thought,.and invented what I conceived to be the appropriate title of "Agnostic." It came into my head as suggestively antithetic to the "Gnostic" of Church history, who professed to know so much about the very things of which I was ignorant; and I took the earliest opportunity of parading it at our Society to show that I, too, had a tail like the other foxes. To my great satisfaction, the term took; and when the *Spectator* had stood godfather to it, any suspicion in the minds of respectable people that a knowledge of its parentage might have awakened was, of course, completely lulled.

Of his share in the debates the late Prof. Henry Sidgwick gives the following account :—

There were several members of the Society with whose philosophical views I had, on the whole, more sympathy ; but there was certainly no one to whom I found it more ˊpleasant and more instructive to listen. Indeed, I soon came to the conclusion that there was only one other member of our Society who could be placed on a par with him as a debater, on the subjects discussed at our meetings ; and that was, curiously enough, a man of the most diametrically opposed opinion—W. G. Ward, the well-known advocate of Ultramontanism. Ward was by training, and perhaps by nature, more of a dialectician ; but your father was unrivalled in the clearness, precision, succinctness, and point of his statements, in his complete and ready grasp of his own system of philosophical thought, and the quickness and versatility with which his thought at once assumed the right attitude of defence against any argument coming from any quarter. I used to think that while others of us could perhaps find, on the spur of the moment, *an* answer more or less effective to some unexpected attack, your father seemed always able to find *the* answer—I mean the answer that it was reasonable to give, consistently with his general view, and much the same answer that he would have given if he had been allowed the fullest time for deliberation.

The general tone of the Metaphysical Society was one of extreme consideration for the feelings of opponents, and your father's speaking formed no exception to the general harmony. At the same time, I seemed to remember him as the most combative of all the speakers who took a leading part in the debates. His habit of never wasting words, and the edge naturally given to his remarks by his genius

for clear and effective statement, partly account for
this impression ; still, I used to think that he liked
fighting, and occasionally liked to give play to his
sarcastic humour—though always strictly within
the limits imposed by courtesy.   I remember that
on one occasion, when I had read to the Society an
essay on " The Incoherence of Empiricism," I looked
forward with some little anxiety to his criticisms ;
and when they came I felt that my anxiety had not
been superfluous ; he " went for " the weak points of
my argument in half-a-dozen trenchant sentences,
of which I shall not forget the impression.   It was
hard hitting, though perfectly courteous and fair.

The paper to be read at each meeting of the Society
was printed and circulated in advance, so that all might
be prepared with their arguments.   Discussion followed
the dinner at which the members met.   Of these papers
Huxley contributed three, the titles of which sufficiently
indicate the fundamental points on which his criticism
played, questioning current axioms in its search for
trustworthy evidence of their validity.   The first (1869)
was on " The Views of Hume, Kant, and Whately on the
Logical Basis of the Doctrine of the Immortality of the
Soul," showing that these thinkers agreed in holding
that no such basis is given by reasoning apart, for
instance, from revelation.   The argument is summarized
in the essay on Hume (*Coll. Ess.*, vi, 201 ; 1878).

The second was " Has a Frog a Soul? and if so, of
what Nature is that Soul?" (1870), a physiological discussion as to the seat of those purposive actions of which
the animal is capable after it has lost ordinary volition
and consciousness by the removal of the front part of its
brain.   Are these things attributes of the soul, and are
they resident not even in the brain, but in the spinal
marrow ?   If metaphysics starts from psychology,
psychology itself depends greatly upon physiology ;

current theories need reconsideration. This paper was the starting-point for his larger essay on "Animals as Automata," delivered as an address before the British Association in 1874.

The third paper (1876) was on "The Evidence of the Miracle of the Resurrection," as to which he, so to say, moved the previous question, arguing that there was no valid evidence of actual death having taken place. The paper was the result of an invitation on the part of some of his metaphysical opponents. As he rejected the miraculous, they asked him to write on a definite miracle, and explain his reasons for not accepting it. He chose this subject because, in the first place, it was a cardinal instance ; and, in the second, that as it was a miracle not worked by Christ himself, a discussion of its genuineness could not possibly suggest personal fraud and so inflict gratuitous pain upon believers in it. The question of the fundamentals of Christian evidences had long been in his mind ; it was no new subject to him when in the eighties, debarred by his health from physiological researches, he extended his work on Biblical studies.

If the Metaphysical Society effected nothing else, it brought about a personal *rapprochement* between the representatives of opposing schools of thought. It became clear to the older school that the new thinkers had by no means failed, as they suspected, to examine the older doctrines. Theirs was not dishonest doubt, but a strong demand for better evidence. If the Society itself "died of too much love," it may well have contributed to the greater amenity of public discussion as the years passed, and the diminution of the former rabid denunciations which waned as the new doctrines spread, and were even absorbed and digested by their former antagonists.

VII

CONTROVERSY AND THE BATTLE OF THE "ORIGIN"

THE piercing clearness of mind described by Prof. Sidgwick, which could not express itself otherwise than trenchantly and drove straight at the heart of the subject, gave Huxley the popular reputation of being above all things a controversialist. Naturally enough, the public knew little and cared less for the unspectacular researches among the Invertebrates, which had won such high scientific fame. They were only stirred when the results of study in geology, in fossil forms and simian anatomy, clashed with long-established popular conceptions. There was also a gladiatorial delight in watching controversy not simply abstract, but fanned by personal conviction, which marked the champions above all as good fighters.

It must be noted, however, that, vigorous as he was in carrying war into the enemy's country, on two occasions only did Huxley set forth without being first personally attacked. One was his review of the *Vestiges of Creation*, when he was irritated by the writer's "prodigious ignorance and thoroughly unscientific habit of mind."

> If it had any influence on me at all [he writes], it set me against Evolution; and the only review I ever have qualms of conscience about, on the ground of needless savagery, is one I wrote on the *Vestiges* while under that influence (1854).

The other was his controversy in 1885–6 with Mr. Gladstone, over the account of the creation in Genesis.

37

But, at least, this was a reply to Mr. Gladstone's attack upon M. Réville and his applications of scientific methods to the problem.

Nevertheless, in this and the similar controversies on Biblical subjects, his chief aim was not simply to confute his adversary. To demolish once more the legend of the Flood, or the literal truth of the Creation myth, in which a multitude of scholars and critics and educated people generally had ceased to believe, was not an otiose slaying of the slain. It made people think of the wider questions involved. To riddle the story of the Gadarene swine was to make a breach in the whole demonology of the New Testament and its claims to superior knowledge of the spiritual world.

It may be noted in passing that, however hard he hit in these controversies, he never descended to anything which would merely wound and offend cherished convictions. His own feelings forbade ribaldry, and abuse disgusted him, on whichever side employed. He declined to admit that rightful freedom of discussion is attacked when a man is prevented from coarsely and brutally insulting his neighbours' honest beliefs. And this apart from the question of bad policy, inasmuch as abuse stultifies argument. But if prosecutions for blasphemy are permitted, it would be but just to penalize some of the anti-scientific blasphemers for their coarse and unmannerly attacks on opinions worthy of all respect.

For the rest, as he humorously remarks, when he began in early days to push his researches into the history and origin of the world and its life, he invariably ran up against a sign-board with the notice, "No Thoroughfare — By Order — Moses." Geology and Biology were shut in by a ring-fence; the universe beyond was a Forbidden Land, guarded by the Lamas of ecclesiastical authority.

The first great clash with this authority, which focussed attention upon the scientific struggle for freedom of thought, was that which followed the publication of the *Origin of Species* at the end of 1859, and culminated in the debate with the Bishop of Oxford at the Oxford meeting of the British Association in 1860. A fierce but more limited struggle for freedom of criticism within the pale of the Church was to follow the publication of *Essays and Reviews* (1860) and Bishop Colenso's examination of the Pentateuch in 1862 and onwards.

The first of these episodes was to have the widest consequences on thought at large. Huxley early had an opportunity of commending the book to the public. The reviewer of the *Times*, knowing nothing about the subject, was advised to entrust the work to him, adding only the opening paragraphs himself. But it was his retort to the Bishop of Oxford six months later which publicly proclaimed how boldly the challenge of authority was to be taken up. The story is well known; how the Bishop came down on the last day of the Association meeting to "smash Darwin." Crowds gathered to hear the great orator, who was also reputed to carry scientific weight as having taken a high mathematical degree. He knew nothing directly of the subject, but apparently had been coached up, somewhat inadequately, by Owen, his guest at Cuddesdon, who did not put in an appearance at the meeting that day, but whose hand was also apparent in the Bishop's *Quarterly* article that was published a few days later.

After several merely rhetorical speakers had been cut short by the chairman, Henslow, who ruled that scientific discussion alone was in order, the Bishop rose in response to calls from the audience, and "spoke for full half-an-hour with inimitable spirit, emptiness, and unfairness," wrote Hooker.

He ridiculed Darwin badly and Huxley savagely ;
but all in such dulcet tones, so persuasive a manner,
and in such well-turned periods, that I, who had been
inclined to blame the President for allowing a discussion that could serve no scientific purpose, now
forgave him from the bottom of my heart.......In a
light, scoffing tone, florid and fluent, he assured us
there was nothing in the idea of evolution ; rock-
pigeons were what rock-pigeons had always been.
Then, turning to his antagonist with a smiling
insolence, he begged to know was it through his
grandfather or his grandmother that he claimed his
descent from a monkey.

Here the Bishop left the vantage ground of any
pretence to scientific discussion, and descended to taste-
less personalities.   Here was the opportunity for an
equally personal retort, which would show an audience,
for the most part neither of a mind nor of a mood to
follow closely argued reasonings, that personalities were
not argument, and that ridicule is a two-edged weapon.
As he spoke these words Huxley turned to Sir Benjamin
Brodie, who was sitting next him, and whispered : " The
Lord hath delivered him into mine hands."

The Bishop sat down ; but Huxley, though directly
attacked, did not rise until the meeting called for him.
Then he "slowly and deliberately arose; a slight, tall
figure, stern and pale, very quiet and very grave."   He
began with a general statement in defence of Darwin's
theory.   " I am here only in the interests of science, and
I have not heard anything which can prejudice the case
of my august client."   Darwin's theory was an explanation of phenomena in Natural History, as the undulatory
theory was of the phenomena of light.   No one objected
to the latter because an undulation of light had never
been arrested and measured.   Darwin offered an explanation of facts, and his book was full of new facts, all

bearing on his theory. Without asserting that every part of that theory had been confirmed, he maintained that it was the best explanation of the origin of species which had yet been offered. As to the psychological distinction between men and animals, and the question of the Creation: "You say that development drives out the Creator; but you assert that God made you: and yet you know that you yourself were originally a little piece of matter no bigger than the end of this gold pencil-case." Nobody could say at what moment of the history of his development man became consciously intelligent. The whole question was not so much one of a transmutation or transition of species as of the production of forms which became permanent. The Ancon sheep was not produced gradually; it originated in the birth of the original parent of the whole stock, which had been kept up by a rigid system of artificial selection.

But if the question were to be treated, not as a matter for the calm investigation of science, but as a matter of sentiment, and if he were asked whether he would choose to be descended from the poor animal of low intelligence and stooping gait who grins and chatters as we pass, or from a man endowed with great ability and a splendid position, who should use these gifts to discredit and crush humble seekers after truth, he must hesitate what answer to make.

The actual words were not taken down at the time; they were finely eloquent, and gained effect from the clear, deliberate utterance; but the nearest approach to them was recorded in a letter of J. R. Green, the future historian, written immediately after the meeting:—

> I asserted—and I repeat—that a man has no reason to be ashamed of having an ape for his grandfather. If there were an ancestor whom I should feel shame in recalling, it would rather be a

D

man—a man of restless and versatile intellect—who, not content with (an equivocal[1]) success in his own sphere of activity, plunges into scientific questions with which he has no real acquaintance, only to obscure them by an aimless rhetoric, and distract the attention of his hearers from the real point at issue by eloquent digressions and skilled appeals to religious prejudice.

The effect was electrical. When he first rose to speak he had been coldly received—no more than a cheer of encouragement from his immediate friends. As he made his points the applause grew. When he finished one half of the audience burst into a storm of cheers; the other was thunderstruck by the sacrilegious recoil of the Bishop's weapon upon his own head : a lady fainted, and had to be carried out. As soon as calm was restored Hooker leapt to his feet, though he hated public speaking yet more than his friend, and drove home the main scientific arguments with his own experience on the botanical side. The Bishop, be it recorded, bore no malice. Orator and wit as he was, he no doubt appreciated a debater whose skill in fence matched his own.

---

[1] Referring to this letter afterwards, my father felt certain that he had never used the word "equivocal." In this he was borne out by Prof. Victor Carus and Prof. Farrar, who were present.

VIII

PUBLIC SPEAKING AND LECTURES

FOR Huxley, one result of the affair was that he became universally known, and not merely as he had been known to his immediate circle, as the most vigorous defender of Darwin—" Darwin's bulldog," as he playfully called himself. Another result was that he changed his idea as to the practical value of the art of public speaking. Walking away from the meeting with that other hater of speech-making, Hooker, he declared that he would thenceforth carefully cultivate it, and try to leave off hating it. The former resolution he carried out faithfully, with the result that he became one of the best speakers of his generation ; in the latter he never quite succeeded. The nervous horror before making a public address seldom wholly left him ; he used to say that when he stepped on the platform at the Royal Institution and heard the door click behind him, he knew what it must be like to be a condemned man stepping out to the gallows. Happily, no sign of nervousness ever showed itself ; he gave the appearance of being equally master of himself and of his subject. His voice was not strong, but he had early learnt the lesson of clear enunciation. There were two letters he received when he began lecturing, and which he kept by him as a perpetual reminder, labelled " Good Advice." One was from a " working man " of his Monday evening audience in Jermyn Street, in 1855 ; the other, undated, from Mr. Jodrell, a great benefactor of science, who had heard him at the Royal Institution. These warned him against his habits of lecturing in a colloquial tone, which might suit a knot of students gathered round his table, but not a large audience ; of running his words, especially technical terms, together, and of pouring out unfamiliar matter at breakneck speed. These early faults were so glaring that one institute in St. John's Wood, after hearing him, petitioned " not to have that young man again." He worked hard to cure himself, and the later audiences who flocked to his lectures could never have guessed at his early failings. The flow was as clear and even as the arrangement of the matter was lucid ; the voice was not loud, but so distinct that it carried to the furthest benches. No syllable was slurred, no point hurried over. All this made for the lucid and comprehensible ; well-chosen language and fine utterance shaped a perfect vehicle of thought. But it was the lucidity of the thought itself, thus expressed, that gave his lectures their quality. A clever and accomplished lady once, in intimate conversation, asked Mrs. Huxley what the reason could be that every one praised her husband so highly as a lecturer. " I can't understand it. He just lets the subject explain itself, and that's all." Profound, if unintended, compliment. It was his power of seeing things clearly, stripped of their non-essentials, that enabled him to make others see them clearly also. Nor did he forget the saying of that prince of popular expositors, Faraday, who, when asked, " How much may a popular lecturer suppose his audience knows ? " replied emphatically, " Nothing." This same faculty, no doubt, was that which enabled him to write such admirable elementary text-books—a task which he regarded as one of the most difficult possible.

A notable description of his public lecturing in the seventies and early eighties is given by G. W. Smalley, correspondent of the *New York Tribune*, in his " London Letters " :—

From a Photograph by Maull and Polyblank, 1857

To face p. 44

I used always to admire the simple and business-
like way in which Huxley made his entry on great
occasions.   He hated anything like display, and
would have none of it.   At the Royal Institution,
more than almost anywhere else, the lecturer, on
whom the concentric circles of spectators in their
steep amphitheatre look down, focuses the gaze.
Huxley never seemed aware that anybody was
looking at him.   From self-consciousness he was,
here as elsewhere, singularly free, as from self-
assertion.   He walked in through the door on the
left as if he were entering his own laboratory.   In
these days he bore scarcely a mark of age.   He was
in the full vigour of manhood, and looked the man he
was......With a firm step and easy bearing he took
his place, apparently without a thought of the people
who were cheering him.   To him it was an anni-
versary.   He looked, and he probably was, the
master.   Surrounded as he was by the celebrities
of science and the ornaments of London drawing-
rooms, there was none who had quite the same kind
of intellectual ascendancy which belonged to him.
The square forehead, the square jaw, the tense lines
of the mouth, the deep, flashing dark eyes, the impression of something more than strength he gave you, an
impression of sincerity, of solid force, of immov-
ability, yet with the gentleness arising from the
serene   consciousness   of   his   strength—all   this
belonged to Huxley, and to him alone.   The first
glance magnetized his audience.   The eyes were
those of one accustomed to command, of one having
authority, and not fearing on occasion to use it.
The hair swept carelessly away from the broad
forehead and   grew   rather   long   behind, yet the
length did not suggest, as it often does, effeminacy.
He was masculine in everything—look, gesture,
speech.   Sparing of gesture, sparing of emphasis,
careless of mere rhetorical or oratorical art, he had,
nevertheless, the secret of the highest art of all,
whether   in   oratory   or   whatever   else—he   had

simplicity. The force was in the thought and the
diction, and he needed no other. The voice was
rather deep, low, but quite audible; at times
sonorous, and always full......His manner here, in
the presence of this select and rather limited
audience—for the theatre of the Royal Institution
holds, I think, less than a thousand people—was
exactly the same as before a great company whom he
addressed at Liverpool, as President of the British
Association for the Advancement of Science.   I
remember going late to that and having to sit far
back, yet hearing every word easily; and there, too,
the feeling was the same—that he had mastered his
audience, taken possession of them, and held them
to the end in an unrelaxing grip, as a great actor at
his best does.   There was nothing of the actor about
him, except that he knew how to stand still; but
masterful he ever was.

Equally perfect of their kind were his class lectures,
which made a deep and lasting impression on his
students.   In the words of Jeffery Parker, afterwards his
assistant :—

His lectures were like his writings, luminously
clear, without the faintest disposition to descend to
the level of his audience; eloquent, but with no
trace of the empty rhetoric which so often does duty
for that quality; full of a high seriousness, but with
no suspicion of pedantry; lightened by an occasional
epigram or flashes of caustic humour, but with none
of the small jocularity in which it is such a tempta-
tion to a lecturer to indulge.   As one listened to him
one felt that comparative anatomy was worthy of
the devotion of a life, and that to solve a morphological problem was as fine a thing as to win a
battle.   He was an admirable draughtsman, and his
blackboard illustrations were always a great feature
of his lectures, especially when, to show the relation
of two animal types, he would, by a few rapid
strokes and smudges, evolve the one into the other

before our eyes. He seemed to have a real affection
for some of the specimens illustrating his lectures,
and would handle them in a peculiarly loving
manner. When he was lecturing on man, for
instance, he would sometimes throw his arm over
the shoulder of the skeleton beside him and take its
hand, as if its silent companionship were an inspiration. To me, his lectures before his small class at
Jermyn Street or South Kensington were almost
more impressive than the discourses at the Royal
Institution, where, for an hour and a-half, he poured
forth a stream of dignified, earnest, sincere words in
perfect literary form, and without the assistance of
a note.

It was no wonder that he was clear and exact in his
class lectures, for he based what he had to say on his
own experiment and observation, and was at pains to
verify experimentally the observations of others which
came within his field. Without verification he would
not rely upon them. Indeed, he was so careful to give
nothing at second hand that one of his scientific friends
gently reproached him for wasting his time in re-investi-
gating matters already worked over by competent
observers. " Poor ——," he remarked afterwards, "if
that is his own practice, his work will never live." Of his
most important public addresses, two may be noted as
especial *tours de force*. On each occasion it was specially
necessary to speak by the book, but at the last moment
it was impossible to use the carefully prepared notes.
One was the address on the complex and difficult subject
of " Animals as Automata," at the Belfast meeting of the
British Association in 1874, when the atmosphere was
electrical after a Presidential address by John Tyndall
which set theologians in an uproar. Years afterwards he
described the incident to Sir E. Ray Lankester :—

I knew that I was treading on very dangerous

ground, so I wrote out uncommonly full and careful notes, and had them in my hand when I stepped on to the platform.

Then I suddenly became aware of the bigness of the audience, and the conviction came upon me that, if I looked at my notes, not one half would hear me. It was a bad ten seconds, but I made my election and turned the notes face downwards on the desk.

To this day I do not exactly know how the thing managed to roll itself out; but it did, as you say, for the best part of an hour and a-half.

There's a story *pour vous encourager* if you are ever in a like fix.

The other was his address at the opening of the John Hopkins University at Baltimore in 1876. Late on the preceding afternoon he returned very tired from an expedition to Washington, to find that a formal dinner and reception awaited him in the evening. He snatched an hour or two of rest, when a New York reporter arrived demanding the text of the address, which had to be sent to New York for simultaneous publication with the Baltimore papers. Now the address was not written out; it was to be delivered from notes only. From these notes, then, he delivered it *in extenso* to the reporter, who took it down in shorthand, and promised to let him have a copy to lecture from next morning. But the fair copy did not come till the last moment. To his horror he found this was written out upon "flimsy," from which it would be impossible to read properly. Again he turned it down on the desk and boldly trusted to memory. This second version was taken down verbatim by the Baltimore reporters in their turn. What if it did not tally with the New York version? As a matter of fact, it was almost identical, save for a few curious discrepancies, apparent contradictions between professed eye-witnesses which the ingenious critic might perfectly well use to prove that both accounts were fictitious, and that the pretended original was never delivered under the conditions alleged.

Mention has been made of his lectures to working men. Of these his assistant and successor, Professor G. B. Howes, wrote :—

> Great as were his class lectures, his working-men's were greater. Huxley was a great believer in the *distillatio per ascensum* of scientific knowledge and culture, and spared no pains in approaching the artisan and so-called "working classes." He gave the workmen of his best. The substance of his *Man's Place in Nature*, one of the most successful and popular of his writings, and of his *Crayfish*, perhaps the most perfect zoological treatise ever published, was first communicated to them. In one of the last conversations I had with him, I asked his views on the desirability of discontinuing the workmen's lectures at Jermyn Street, since the development of working men's colleges and institutes is regarded by some to have rendered their continuance unnecessary. He replied, almost with indignation : " With our central position and resources, we ought to be in a position to give the workmen that which they cannot get elsewhere " ; adding that he would deeply deplore any such discontinuance.

He had begun these in 1855, the second year of his appointment at the Royal School of Mines. On February 27 of that year he wrote to his friend Dr. Dyster :—

> I enclose a prospectus of some People's Lectures (*Popular* Lectures I hold to be an abomination unto the Lord) I am about to give here. I want the working classes to understand that Science and her ways are great facts for them—that physical virtue is the base of all other, and that they are to be clean and temperate and all the rest, not because fellows in black with white ties tell them so, but

> because these are plain and patent laws of nature
> which they must obey "under penalties."
>
> I am sick of the *dilettante* middle class, and mean
> to try what I can do with these hard-handed fellows
> who live among facts.

And in May, after referring to his Preliminary Course
and the earnestness and attention of his audience, he
adds that he has begun his similar course to working
men exclusively—a series of six, given in turn by each
Professor :—

> The theatre holds 600, and is crammed full. I
> believe in the fustian, and can talk better to it than
> to any amount of gauze and Saxony; and to
> a fustian audience (but to that only) I would
> willingly give some when I come to Tenby [Dr.
> Dyster's home].

Moreover, he took a practical interest in the corre-
sponding movement set afoot by F. D. Maurice, and
gave occasional addresses at the Working Men's College
between 1857 and 1877, the last of which was that
delightful discourse on science as "trained and organized
common sense" which bears the alluring title of "The
Method of Zadig."

IX

POPULAR EDUCATION

THESE lectures to working men, no less than his profound interest and exhausting work on behalf of popular education, illustrate his intense belief that science is not solely a thing of the laboratory, but a vital factor in right living. It was still true that the people perish for want of knowledge. And as he said when talking of posthumous fame : " If I am to be remembered at all, I should like to be remembered as one who did his best to help the people."

Nor did he lack appreciation among those whom he tried thus to aid. Professor Mivart tells the following story :—

> I recollect going [in 1874] with him and Mr. John Westlake, Q.C., to a meeting of artisans in the Blackfriars Road, to whom he gave a friendly address. He felt a strong interest in working men, and was much beloved by them. On one occasion, having taken a cab home, on his arrival there, when he held out his fare to the cabman, the latter replied : "Oh no, Professor ; I have had too much pleasure and profit from hearing you lecture to take any money from your pocket ; proud to have driven you, Sir ! "

Another story is told by Mr. Raymond Blaythwayt :—

> Only to-day I had a most striking instance of sentiment come beneath my notice. I was about to enter my house, when a plain, simply dressed working man came up to me with a note in his hand, and, touching his hat, he said : " I think this is for you,

51

Sir"; and then he added : "Will you give me the
envelope, Sir, as a great favour?" I looked at it,
and, seeing it bore the signature of Professor
Huxley, I replied : "Certainly I will ; but why do
you ask for it?" "Well," said he ; "it's got
Professor Huxley's signature, and it will be something for me to show my mates and keep for my
children. He has done me and my like a lot of
good ; no man more."

In these special lectures of his very best and in his
other essays, which, however far-reaching, were always
intelligible to plain readers, may be seen one side of his
desire to spread clear thinking among the less instructed
masses ; another was his work on the first School Board.
By 1870 his health was already shaken by the heavy
work which filled his days and nights ; nevertheless,
whatever the cost in time and labour and health, he felt
it imperative to try, with all his power, to give rational
shape to the new lines of universal education, and to
revivify it with the fresh breath of the new renascence
in aim and method. Science must be represented in the
new Parliament of Education, and there was no one else
ready to undertake the part. Moreover, he had already
enjoyed some practical experience of the workings of
elementary education while examiner under the Science
and Art Department, the establishment of which he
considered

a measure which came into existence unnoticed, but
which will, I believe, turn out to be of more importance to the welfare of the people than many
political changes over which the noise of battle has
rent the air.

On the proper working of the new Act depended the
physical, moral, and intellectual betterment of the
nation ; in particular, "book-learning" needed to be
tempered with not merely handcraft, but with something

of the direct knowledge of nature ; for in itself, if properly
applied, this is an admirable instrument of education, and
by its method promotes an attitude of mind capable of
understanding the reasons for the vast changes at work
in human thought.

Accordingly, he stood as a candidate for Marylebone,
and, without canvassing, for which he had neither time
nor inclination, he was elected second on the list.   He
had addressed several meetings, and, as an amplification
of his election address, he included extracts from his
forthcoming article, " The School Boards : What They
Can Do, and What They May Do," which were sent to the
papers by the editor of the *Contemporary Review*.   (See
Coll. Ess., iii, 374.)   Here was his programme, a great
part of which he saw carried out :—Physical training,
for health and as a basis for further training ; Domestic
training, especially for girls ; Moral training, in a knowledge of moral and social laws, and an engaging of the
affections for what is good instead of what is evil ;
Intellectual training, in knowledge and the means of
acquiring knowledge, alike for practical purposes and for
recreation.

The opponents of popular education raised their still
familiar outcry about " cramming children full of nonsense " and " unfitting them for the state of life to which
they were called."   But one cannot say what state of
life they may be called to without opportunity of testing
their capacities, and as for cramming them with nonsense, such a scheme, if properly carried out, ought
rather to expel nonsense.   Above all, it set the interests
of humanity above the mere development of skill, which
would simply turn the child of man into the subtlest
beast of the field.

True education, he declared, was impossible without
" religion," the unchanging essence of which lies in the

love of some ethical ideal to govern and guide conduct, "together with the awe and reverence which have no kinship with base fear, but rise whenever one tries to pierce below the surface of things, whether they be material or spiritual."

It was in this sense that he advocated Bible-reading in schools—simple Bible-reading, without theological gloss. On the one hand, this was the only workable plan under existing circumstances. True, that he would not have employed the Bible as the agency for introducing the religious and ethical idea in a system that could begin with a clean slate. He believed that the principle of strict secularity in State education is sound and must ultimately prevail. But moral instruction must not be too rudely divorced from the system of belief current among the generality ; and the Bible had been the instrument of the clergy of all denominations, to whose efforts the mass of half-instructed people owed such redemption from ignorance and barbarism as they possessed. Make all needful deductions, and there remains a vast residuum of moral beauty and grandeur, interwoven with three centuries of our history. The Bible, as English literature, as old-world history, as moral teaching, as the Magna Charta of the poor and of the oppressed, the most democratic book in the world, could not be spared. The mass of the people should not be deprived of the one great literature which is open to them ; not shut out from the perception of their relations with the whole past history of civilized mankind, nor from an unpriestly view of Judaism and Jesus of Nazareth, purged of the accretions of centuries. Accordingly, he supported Mr. W. H. Smith's motion for Bible-reading, even against the champions of immediate secularization ; but for Bible-reading under such regulations as would carry out for the children the intention of Mr. W. E. Forster, the originator of the Education Act, that "in the reading and explanation of the Bible......no efforts will be made to cram into their poor little minds theological dogmas which their tender age prevents them from understanding."

But the compromise was not permanently satisfactory. In 1893–94 the clerical party on the School Board "denounced" the treaty agreed to in 1871, and up till then undisputed, in the expectation of securing a new one more favourable to themselves; and the *Times*, hurrying to their support, did not hesitate to declare in a leading article that "the persons who framed the rule" respecting religious instruction intended to include definite teaching of such theological dogmas as the Incarnation.

In a letter to the *Times* Huxley replied (April 29, 1893) :—

> I cannot say what may have been in the minds of the framers of the rule; but, assuredly, if I had dreamed that any such interpretation could fairly be put upon it, I should have opposed the arrangement to the best of my ability.
>
> In fact, a year before the rule was framed I wrote an article in the *Contemporary Review*, entitled "The School Boards—what they can do and what they may do," in which I argued that the terms of the Education Act excluded such teaching as it is now proposed to include.

And this contention he supported by the quotation from Mr. W. E. Forster, given above.

Further, in October, 1894, he replied as follows to a correspondent who had asked him whether flat adhesion to the compromise had not made nonsense of a certain Bible lesson, which was the subject of much comment :—

> I am at one with you in hating "hush up" as I do all other forms of lying; but I venture to submit that the compromise of 1871 was not a "hush up." If I had taken it to be such, I should have refused to have anything to do with it......

There has never been the slightest ambiguity about my position in the matter; in fact, if you will turn to one paper on the School Board written by me before my election in 1870, I think you will find that I anticipated the pith of the present discussion.

The persons who agreed to the compromise did exactly what all sincere men who agree to compromise do. For the sake of the enormous advantage of giving the rudiments of a decent education to several generations of the people, they accepted what was practically an armistice in respect of certain matters about which the contending parties were absolutely irreconcilable.

To return to his activity on the School Board. His vigorous work as chairman of the committee appointed to frame an educational scheme was marked by great breadth of view. He desired the elementary schools to be linked at the one end with infant schools; at the other with continuation schools and some scheme for technical education. A perfect scheme would provide what he first called a ladder from the gutter to the university, whereby children of exceptional capacity might reach the places for which nature had fitted them. His sense of fitness would have welcomed even more warmly some system whereby the incompetent born into the higher strata of the social organism should be automatically graded down to the positions more appropriate to their wits and character. But this is an ideal only possible in Plato's State, where philosophers are kings and possess superhuman power of intuition.

Sincerity is sometimes impracticable. But here sincerity was combined with common-sense practicality, and even an opponent like Lord Shaftesbury was impelled to write in his journal:—" Professor Huxley has this definition of morality and religion : ' Teach a child what is wise : that is *morality*. Teach him what is wise and beautiful: that is *religion!*' Let no one henceforth despair of making things ᐯlear and of giving explanations!"

He did not, however, disguise his fundamental opposition to Ultramontanism, that intellectual and social *imperium in imperio*, with its basic hostility to the free scientific spirit. This he had already expressed in his "Scientific Education" (*Coll. Ess.*, iii, 111), an address of 1869, and he repeated it towards the end of his service on the School Board when opposing a bye-law that the Board should pay over direct to denominational schools the fees for poor children—to schools, that is, outside the Board's control. He opposed it partly because it would assuredly lead to repeated contests on the Board; partly because it would give a handle to that party whose system, as set forth in the syllabus, of securing complete possession of the minds of their flock, was destructive of all that was highest in the nature of mankind and inconsistent with intellectual and political liberty.

The committee did excellent work in systematizing important matters and leaving minor arrangements to the local managers; in apportioning essential and discretionary subjects, and—what was of special interest to its chairman—the teaching of elementary geography and elementary social economy, and in particular the systematized object-lessons, embracing a course of elementary construction in physical science, and serving as an introduction to the courses for the examinations under the Science and Art Department. Science, as he declared, was assuming such a position alike in practical life and in thought that any one totally ignorant of it would be at a disadvantage in both spheres. Moreover, the proposed technical schools—for applied science, that is—must suffer if they had to deal with pupils who had

E

no preliminary grounding in the principles of physical science. His early advocacy of music and drawing, not to produce artists, but to develop personality, also bore some fruit. The man of science, too, was found defending Latin as a discretionary subject, alternatively with a modern language. Latin was the gate to many things, and, apart from the question of overloading the curriculum, there was great danger if educational possibilities were not thrown open to all without restriction. There is no more frightful " sitting on the safety valve " than in denying men of ability the means of rising to the positions for which their talents and industry might qualify them.

As for the compulsory element in education and the justification for levying rates and taxes for what objectors called "educating other people's children," his answer was : " Every ignorant person tends to become a burden upon, and, so far, an infringer of the liberty of, his fellows, and an obstacle to their success. Under such circumstances an education rate is, in fact, a war tax, levied for purposes of defence."

In all this it was his attitude towards the child which deeply impressed his colleagues in whom child-sympathy was strongest. As the Rev. Benjamin Waugh put it, he was on the Board to establish schools for the children. He wanted to turn them into sound men and women, and resented the idea that schools were to train either congregations for churches or hands for factories. " What he sought to do for the child was for the child's sake, that it might live a fuller, truer, worthier life."

After fifteen months of service on the School Board superadded to the heavy strain of his ordinary work, his health broke down utterly, and he resigned. But after his retirement his successors found that their duty was " to put into practice the scheme of instruction which

Huxley was mainly instrumental in settling. We were thus able indirectly to improve both the means and methods of teaching......The most important developments and additions have been in the direction of educating the hand and eye......Thus the impulse given by Huxley in the first months of the Board's existence has been carried forward by others." So wrote Dr. J. H. Gladstone in 1896. The tide of education has swelled since then and is still swelling, but its main direction is the same.

NOTE

As these pages are passing through the press, I note an appeal for money by the Religious Tract Society, which is running short of funds to keep up the number and quality of the 6–7,000 Bibles annually awarded as prizes to elementary school children. This advertisement fills more than half a column of the *Times* of March 25, 1920. It is headed in bold type, PROFESSOR HUXLEY ON THE BIBLE, and, opening with the words " All who value the teaching of the Holy Bible will appreciate this wonderful description of the Bible by Professor Huxley," proceeds to quote the eloquent passage, referred to above on p. 54, from "The School Boards, etc." (*Coll. Ess.*, iii, 396).

This testimony to the interest of the Bible outside its theological applications is detached from its context as a spur to " all those who value the Word of God......to send the Society help in [its] work of extending Bible teaching in our Elementary Schools."

But these words were written with grave qualifications, especially as to the need of excluding doctrinal teaching. By suppressing these qualifications the Secretaries of the Religious Tract Society approve themselves denizens of the world of half-truths, along with puff-writers and similar experts.

X

EDUCATION: ESPECIALLY OF TEACHERS
AND OF WOMEN

THE third of his excursions into the field of education, in his burning desire to give the people that right knowledge for want of which they perish, was the training of the teachers who prepared pupils for the examinations of the Science and Art Department. The future of scientific teaching depended upon the proper supply of trained teachers. Now, the School of Mines in Jermyn Street was without a laboratory in which to make even his own students work out with their own hands the structure of the biological "types" expounded in the lectures. An opportunity to train these new "scientific missionaries" came in 1871, when he was deep in the great schemes of elementary education. More than a hundred of them flocked to South Kensington, where some large rooms on the ground floor of the museum had been secured and rigged up for the purpose by the Professor and his three demonstrators. For six weeks in the summer there was a daily lecture, followed by four hours' laboratory work under the demonstrators, in which the students verified for themselves facts which they had hitherto heard about and taught to their unfortunate pupils from books alone. The naïve astonishment and delight of the more intelligent among them was sometimes almost pathetic. One clergyman, who had for years conducted classes in physiology under the Science and Art Department, was shown a drop of his own blood under the microscope. "Dear me!"

he exclaimed, "it's just like the picture in Huxley's *Physiology*."

From 1872 onwards, when the School of Mines removed bodily to new buildings at South Kensington, Huxley had a fine laboratory of his own, in which not only were these teachers taught, but he was able to adopt the same method with the students in his regular courses—a method for long universally adopted in detail as well as in principle. The first and unchangeable principle was to make the student verify every fact for himself; to be satisfied with nothing at second hand. The system was to work over a chosen set of biological types, each representing a well-marked group and providing comparisons one with another as well as stepping-stones to further investigations. Originally he started the series with the simplest organisms, and proceeded to the more complex; but, though a good philosophical order, it had the disadvantages of requiring the beginner to have much skill in handling the microscope, and of proceeding from the less known organism to the better known. Starting with the latter, the beginner would know better what to look for. His demonstrator, Jeffery Parker, argued the point vigorously with Huxley, and finally persuaded him to invert the series, with great success, albeit other lecturers preferred to keep to his original arrangement.

Education, furthermore, owes him a great debt for his long and active work upon the Royal Commissions on the Royal College of Science for Ireland, on Science and Art Instruction in Ireland, on Scientific Instruction and the Advancement of Science; on Vivisection, to inquire into the Universities of Scotland, and on the Medical Acts—all in the sixteen years between 1866 and 1882. At the London University, also, he was an examiner for many years, and in the early nineties he strove hard to

give it a new constitution, first as a member of the
Senate, and then as president of a reforming Association.
It is noteworthy, too, that ten years earlier he was
elected a Governor of Eton College, and in the short time
before his health broke down a second time he did something to aid science-teaching there and to make drawing
a general subject.

In the general need for education he ranked high the
need for the education of women. As early as 1860 he
wrote : " I don't see how we are to make any permanent
advancement while one-half of the race is sunk, as nine-
tenths of women are, in mere ignorant parsonese super-
stitions."   If only people would not bring up their
daughters as man-traps for the matrimonial market, the
next generation would see women fit to be the companions of men in all their pursuits ; " though," he added,
" I don't think that men have anything to fear from their
competition."   On this point he remarked five years
later : " Nature's old salique law will never be repealed,
and no change of dynasty will be effected, though whatever argument justifies a given education for boys justifies
its application to girls as well."

A letter of 1874, touching the first efforts of women to
qualify as doctors, prefigures what has been done since
for the higher education of women :—

> Without seeing any reason to believe that women
> are, on the average, so strong physically, intel-
> lectually, or morally, as men, I cannot shut my eyes
> to the fact that many women are much better
> endowed in all these respects than many men, and
> I am at a loss to understand on what grounds of
> justice or public policy a career which is open to the
> weakest and most foolish of the male sex should be
> forcibly closed to women of vigour and capacity.
>
> We have heard a great deal lately about the
> physical disabilities of women.   Some of these

alleged impediments, no doubt, are really inherent in their organization, but nine-tenths of them are artificial—the products of their modes of life. I believe that nothing would tend so effectually to get rid of these creations of idleness, weariness, and that " over-stimulation of the emotions " which, in plainer-spoken days, used to be called wantonness, than a fair share of healthy work, directed towards a definite object, combined with an equally fair share of healthy play during the years of adolescence ; and those who are best acquainted with the requirements of an average medical practitioner will find it hardest to believe that the attempt to reach that standard is likely to prove exhausting to an ordinarily intelligent and well-educated young woman.

Twenty years later he supported the entry of women into public life in a plainly reasoned letter, which he himself thought highly complimentary, although a number of estimable ladies flew at him for writing it :—

The best of women are apt to be a little weak in the great practical arts of give-and-take and putting up with a beating, and a little too strong in their belief in the efficacy of government.   Men learn about these things in the ordinary course of their business ; women have no chance in home life, and the boards and councils will be capital schools for them.   Again, in the public interest it will be well ; women are more naturally economical than men, and have none of our false shame about looking after pence.   Moreover, they don't job for any but their lovers, husbands, and children, so that we know the worst.

Directly, then, as teacher, lecturer, and essayist indirectly as organizer, he ranks among the great educators of his age.   But he did not establish a " school " of his own ; such a thing was abhorrent to him. A resolute seeker after truth, he bade others seek also ;

but he refused to impose his own conclusions on any man.

> Of all possible positions [he wrote in 1892], that
> of master of a school, or leader of a sect, or chief of
> a party, appears to me to be the most undesirable ;
> in fact, the average British matron cannot look upon
> followers with a more evil eye than I do. Such
> acquaintance with the history of thought as I
> possess has taught me to regard school, parties, and
> sects as arrangements, the usual effect of which is
> to perpetuate all that is worst and feeblest in the
> master's, leader's, or founder's work ; or else, as in
> some cases, to upset it altogether ; as a sort of
> hydrant for extinguishing the fire of genius, and for
> stifling the flame of high aspirations, the kindling of
> which has been the chief, perhaps the only, merit of
> the protagonist of the movement. I have always
> been, am, and propose to remain a mere scholar.
> All that I have ever proposed to myself is to say,
> This and this have I learned, thus and thus have I
> learned it ; go thou and learn better; but do not
> thrust on my shoulders the responsibility for your
> own laziness if you elect to take, on my authority,
> conclusions the value of which you ought to have
> tested for yourself.

In fact, what his teaching stood for was not so much
the thing taught as the method by which facts should be
observed and conclusions drawn from them. As science,
in his definition, is but trained and organized common
sense, so this method, the scientific method, is but the
ordinary common-sense method rigidly carried out. And
the correlative to this method is the attitude of mind
that suspends judgment until adequate proof is
forthcoming.

XI

METHODS OF WORK

OF his method of work something has already been said, recalling his insistence upon verifying, experimentally, all statements made by others which he wished to employ in his lectures. This was true not only of his daily teaching, but of any new research that interested him. He repeated the series of Pasteur's experiments for himself before making a pronouncement on the much-debated question of spontaneous generation. A curious by-result of these investigations was that the Admiralty requested him to track down the cause of great trouble in the Navy—namely, that the ship's biscuit, though carefully prepared and packed in tins, was constantly found, when the tins were opened, to be full of maggots.

His far-ranging work in Comparative Anatomy was based upon dissections by his own hand, executed rapidly and broadly, going straight to the essential point without any finikin elaboration, and recorded in very fine anatomical drawings. Indeed, his power of clear and rapid draughtsmanship was the other side of his unusual power of visualizing a conception. Each faculty helped the other, and one of the most striking examples of his memory of forms was when, before a delighted audience, he traced on the blackboard the development of some complex structure, showing, stroke upon stroke, the orderly transition from one form to the next.

Until failing health forbade work with the microscope, he was continually busy with the rational re-grouping of animal forms. Besides his published works on the anatomy of both the Invertebrates and the Vertebrates, whether manuals of anatomy or monographs of special groups or general essays, and his work of classifying birds and reptiles and fishes on new principles, there exists among the vast number of drawings and notes preserved at the Huxley Laboratory at South Kensington a quantity of unpublished and unfinished work which, in detail, often anticipates the work of subsequent investigators, and which, for the most part, represents fresh studies of special groups of animals to be used in a general classification such as was suggested in his paper " On the Application of the Laws of Evolution to the arrangement of the Vertebrata, and more particularly of the Mammalia " (1880)—" the most masterly," remarks Professor Howes, " of his scientific theses ; the only expression which he gave to the world of the interaction of a series of revolutionary ideas and conceptions (begotten of the labours of his closing years as a working zoologist) which were at the period assuming shape in his mind.   They have done more than all else of their period to rationalize the application of our knowledge of the Vertebrata, and have now left their mark for all time on the history of progress, as embodied in our classificatory systems."   But neither this great work nor the other special monographs still in hand reached completion.   His health broke down ; he could no lónger stoop over the microscope, and had perforce to abandon zoological work before he was sixty.

A remark made by Huxley about others is very true of himself—that what matters most is not the microscope, but the man behind it; not the objects seen, but the interpretation of them and their relationships.   The outward and the inward eye had the same quickness, the same highly developed sense of form and relationship, backed by a store of living knowledge; so well organized that it could respond at once to any suggestion which would throw light on undiscovered affinities and provide a true base for classification.

While much of his bookwork and writing was done at home, his later anatomical work was done at his laboratory. As official engagements multiplied, his time was much broken into ; but he snatched every available moment, often dashing down to South Kensington in a cab for a half-hour of work between two official meetings. His absorption in his studies was intense— as at one time he signs himself to his fellow-worker, W. K. Parker, " Ever yours amphibially," so Jeffery Parker, his demonstrator, who tells the story, came to him with a question about the brain of the codfish at a time when he was deep in the investigation of some invertebrate group. " Codfish ? " he replied ; " that's a vertebrate, isn't it ? Ask me a fortnight hence, and I'll consider it."

One more note concerning his method of work. His love of visualizing his problems regularly led him to make charts to show geographically, say, the distribution of certain forms of life over the globe, or to illustrate points of history—such, for example, as a coloured map of the Aegean, with fifty-mile circles drawn from the centre of the Cyclades to illustrate the range of Greek civilization as it spread over the shores of Asia and Europe. And as in writing a book he was careful first to plan out the scheme of it and the balance of the parts, so, however much his public addresses gave the impression of being largely impromptu, he had always thought out carefully every word he meant to say. "There is," he said, "no greater danger than the so-called *inspiration of the moment*, which leads you to say something which is not exactly true, or which you would regret afterwards."

Yet his was not a strong verbal memory. It was essentially a memory for facts; he could tear the heart out of a book as swiftly as a Macaulay, packing the facts into the framework of his knowledge, and always knowing thereafter where to find his facts or verify his references. In his speeches it was the compelling thought seeking expression, and fitting the form of expression exactly to the form of the thought, that brought the meditated words so infallibly and so spontaneously to his lips: they were already welded together in mind. But he had not that kind of memory which, after once reading a page of a book, can recite the whole word for word, whether prose or verse. Single phrases embodying a notable image would remain with him, and remain ready for use as allusive colour or pointed epigram. Many of these were Biblical phrases, for he knew his Bible well, and admired not only the grandeur of thought to be found enshrined in it, but its magnificence as a treasure-house of our English tongue. And, apart from many scientific terms of his invention, he coined divers words and phrases which have enriched our language, such as "Agnostic," "the ladder from the gutter to the university," the descriptions of Positivism as "Catholicism without Christianity," and the Salvation Army methods as "Corybantic Christianity."

His working day began soon after nine, for he was never one of those people who can do hours of work before breakfast. The working day, however, regularly went on until midnight, and, as has been mentioned, was often prolonged by late reading.

The speed with which his mind worked to see through complex questions and spring swiftly to a conclusion was such that he contrived to do four ordinary men's work in a single lifetime. But this swiftness of reaching a conclusion, so useful at most times, was liable some-

times to betray him. If, however, he found that he had
made a mistake, he was ready to confess the fact. The
most celebrated instance of this was the story of
Bathybius. In 1868, while soundings were being made
in connection with the laying of the Atlantic cable,
certain specimens of mud were dredged up. The mud
was sticky, owing to the presence of innumerable lumps
of a transparent gelatinous substance. This was in
fine granules, which possessed neither a nucleus nor
a covering membrane. Scattered through it were cal-
careous coccoliths. Such were the facts; what inference
was to be drawn? The only thing this substance
resembled was one of the many simple forms of oceanic
life recently found and described by the great zoologist
Haeckel.

> I conceive [wrote Huxley] that the granulate heaps
> and the transparent gelatinous matter in which they
> are embedded represent masses of protoplasm. Take
> away the cysts which characterize the *Radiolaria*,
> and a dead *Sphærozoum* would very nearly represent
> one of this deep-sea "Urschleim," which must, I
> think, be regarded as a new form of those simple
> animated beings which have recently been so well
> described by Haeckel in his *Monographie der Moneras.*

So it received the name of Bathybius Haeckelii.

The explanation was plausible enough, if the evidence
had been all that it seemed to be. But the specimens
examined by himself and by Haeckel, who two years
later published a full and detailed description of *Bathybius*,
were seen only in a preserved state. It was dredged up
again on the voyage of the *Porcupine* and examined in
a fresh state by Sir Wyville Thomson and Dr. W. B.
Carpenter, but they found no better explanation to give
of it. Doubt only arose when, in 1879, the *Challenger*
expedition failed to find it very widely distributed, as
expected, over the sea bottom; and the behaviour of

certain specimens gave good ground for suspecting that
what had been sent home before as genuine deep-sea
mud was a precipitate due to the action on the specimens
of the spirit in which they were preserved. Though
Haeckel—his large experience of Monera fortified by the
discovery of a close parallel near Greenland in 1876—
would not desert Bathybius, the rest of its sponsors gave
it up. The evidence in this particular case was tainted.
At the meeting of the British Association in 1879 Huxley
came forward and took occasion to " eat the leek " in a
speech as witty as it was candid.

Now, *Bathybius* had often been pointed to as an
example of almost primordial life, from which the
evolutionary chain might have begun ; and later contro-
versialists, not acquainted with the precise limitations
of the matter, seized upon the *Bathybius* recantation as
a convenient stick with which to beat the Darwinian
dog. To the most noteworthy case of this, eleven years
later, Huxley retorted :—

> That which interested me in the matter was the
> apparent analogy of *Bathybius* with other well-
> known forms of lower life......Speculative hopes or
> fears had nothing to do with the matter, and if
> *Bathybius* were brought up alive from the bottom
> of the Atlantic to-morrow the fact would not have
> the slightest bearing that I can discern upon Mr.
> Darwin's speculations, or upon any of the disputed
> problems of biology.

As to the eating of the leek, he had commended it many
a long year before to an over-impetuous German friend
who had read enough Shakespeare to understand the
meaning of the phrase :—

> Well, every honest man has to do that now and
> then, and I assure you that, if eaten fairly and
> without grimaces, the devouring of that herb has a

very wholesome cooling effect on the blood, particularly in people of a sanguine temperament.

Reflections on making mistakes lead to a striking conclusion :—

> The most considerable difference I note among men is not in their readiness to fall into error, but in their readiness to acknowledge these inevitable lapses.

Until he reached middle age, his quickness of thought and decision was fretted by men of slower mind if they happened to be associated with him on some enterprise, and to certain colleagues his ardour was sometimes almost terrifying. And in those days also, before custom had hardened him, he was apt to be short with those devoid of any claim to intervene who thrust themselves into his affairs. Salutary as this doubtless was to the really ignorant meddler, there was one occasion, of which I learnt thirty years later, where at bottom the rebuke was not deserved. The sufferer, admittedly devoid of anatomical knowledge, questioned the statement in an early edition of *The Elementary Physiology* as to the method in which the voice is produced, and propounded a different movement in part of the larynx. The Professor replied to the effect that the writer had better learn some anatomy before challenging the result of careful experiment. But some years later, as a result of further investigation, this same change was made in a new edition of the book. By that time the very name of the critic was forgotten. But if he and his suggestion had been remembered, I am inclined to think that he would have received an *amende*.

XII

SCIENCE AND ETHICS

HUXLEY'S work in education was his direct contribution to the social improvement of the world. Not instruction merely—for, "though under-instruction is a bad thing, it is not impossible that over-instruction may be a worse " —but through education, the bringing out of the moral worth and intellectual clearness of the individual citizen, which is the one condition of the success of a State. And this condition, resting on the basic faith in veracity, he felt to be above all the work of science, the Cinderella of thought. For, as he wrote :—

> If the diseases of Society consist in the weakness of its faith in the existence of the God of the theologians, in a future state, and in uncaused volitions, the indication, as the doctors say, is to suppress Theology and Philosophy, whose bickerings about things of which they know nothing have been the prime cause and continual sustenance of that evil scepticism which is the Nemesis of meddling with the unknowable.
>
> Cinderella is modestly conscious of her ignorance of these high matters. She lights the fire, sweeps the house, and provides the dinner ; and is rewarded by being told that she is a base creature, devoted to low and material interests. But in her garret she has fairy visions out of the ken of the pair of shrews who are quarrelling downstairs. She sees the order which pervades the seeming disorder of the world ; the great drama of evolution, with its full share of pity and terror, but also with abundant goodness and beauty, unrolls itself before her eyes ; and she

learns, in her heart of hearts, the lesson, that the foundation of morality is to have done, once and for all, with lying; to give up pretending to believe that for which there is no evidence, and repeating unintelligible propositions about things beyond the possibilities of knowledge.

She knows that the safety of morality lies neither in the adoption of this or that philosophical speculation, or this or that theological creed, but in a real and living belief in that fixed order of nature which sends social disorganization upon the track of immorality, as surely as it sends physical disease after physical trespasses. And of that firm and lively faith it is her high mission to be the priestess.

In a world the elements of which are thus mixed with pity and terror, goodness and beauty, he held himself, like the majority of men, as neither optimist nor pessimist. "The world is neither so good, nor so bad, as it conceivably might be; and as most of us have reason, now and again, to discover that it can be."

On the one side, the optimistic dogma that this is the best of all possible worlds is little better than a libel on possibility. On behalf of the modified optimism that benevolence is on the whole the regulating principle of the sentient world, it may be granted that there are hosts of subtle contrivances devoted to the production of pleasure and the avoidance of pain; but, if so, why is it not equally proper to say of the equally numerous arrangements, the no less necessary result of which is the production of pain, that they are evidences of malevolence? Translating these facts into moral terms, the goodness of the hand that aids Blake's "little lamb" is neutralized by the wickedness of the other hand that eggs on his "tiger burning bright," and the course of nature will appear to be neither moral nor immoral, but non-moral.

F

On the other side, though this may not be the best of all possible worlds, to say that it is the worst is "mere petulant nonsense." With a courage based on hours and days of personal knowledge, he exclaims :—

> There can be no doubt in the mind of any reasonable person that mankind could, would, and in fact do, get on fairly well with vastly less happiness and far more misery than find their way into the lives of nine people out of ten. If each and all of us had been visited by an attack of neuralgia, or of extreme mental depression, for one hour in every twenty-four—a supposition which many tolerably vigorous people know, to their cost, is not extravagant—the burden of life would have been immensely increased without much practical hindrance to its general course. Men with any manhood in them find life quite worth living under worse conditions than these.

Moreover, another fact utterly contradicts the hypothesis that the sentient world is directed by malevolence :—

> A vast multitude of pleasures, and these among the purest and the best, are superfluities, bits of good which are, to all appearance, unnecessary as inducements to live, and are, so to speak, thrown into the bargain of life. To those who experience them, few, delights can be more entrancing than such as are afforded by natural beauty, or by the arts, and especially by music ; but they are products of, rather than factors in, evolution, and it is probable that they are known, in any considerable degree, to but a very small proportion of mankind.

To speak, then, of the course and intention of nature in terms of human thought, we must say that its governing principle is intellectual and not moral. It is a logical process materialized, with pleasures and pains that fall, in most cases, without the slightest reference to moral desert.

From the moralist's point of view the animal world, in which our own cosmic nature has been severely trained for millions of years, is no better than a gladiatorial show, and we cannot expect, within a few centuries, to subdue the masterfulness of this inborn tendency, in part necessary to our existence, to purely ethical ends. So deep rooted is it that the struggle may last till the end of time. But, he exclaims with a ringing note—

> I see no limit to the extent to which intelligence and will, guided by sound principles of investigation, and organized in common effort, may modify the conditions of existence for a period longer than that now covered by history. And much may be done to change the nature of man himself. The intelligence which has converted the brother of the wolf into the faithful guardian of the flock ought to be able to do something towards curbing the instincts of savagery in civilized men.

In the long struggle pain and sorrow are inevitable. The aim of man is not to escape these, but rather to earn peace and self-respect. To this he added a special point, in a letter of 1890 : —

> If you will accept the results of the experience of an old man who has had a very chequered existence —and has nothing to hope for except a few years of quiet downhill—there is nothing of permanent value (putting aside a few human affections), nothing that satisfies quiet reflection, except the sense of having worked according to one's capacity and light, to make things clear and get rid of cant and shams of all sorts. That was the lesson I learned from Carlyle's books when I was a boy, and it has stuck by me all my life.

The animal world, then, having the principle of its existence in a state of war, society was created by the first men who substituted the state of mutual peace for the state of mutual war. The object of society was the limitation of the struggle for existence. That shape of society most nearly approaches perfection in which the war of individual against individual is most strictly limited. Happiness and freedom of action are restricted to a sphere where they do not interfere with the happiness and freedom of others ; the common weal becomes an essential part of individual welfare. In short, even if under the most perfect conditions " Witless will always serve his master," man aims to escape from his place in the animal kingdom, founded on the free development of the principle of non-moral evolution, and to establish a kingdom of Man governed upon the principle of moral evolution. For society not only has a moral end, but in its perfection social life is embodied morality. Moral purpose is " an article of exclusively human manufacture —and very much to our credit."

To society, then, its members owe a vital debt ; for society, the work of the ethical man, has slowly and painfully built up around us a fabric of defence against barbarism, the work of the non-ethical man. This debt we are bound to repay by furthering in ourselves the good work of human fellowship, and by striving to improve the conditions of our social life ; and the means thereto are self-discipline, self-support, intelligent effort, not unreasoning violence with its disruption of the defences against anarchic barbarism.

Yet if society, in making life easier, multiplies the species in excess of the means of subsistence, it raises up within itself, in the intensest form, the unlimited struggle for existence. " This is the true riddle of the Sphinx, and every nation which does not solve it will, sooner or later, be devoured by the monster itself has generated."

Improvement there has been during the historical period : with goodwill and clear thought Huxley looked for ever-accelerating improvement, though contemporary

civilizations seemed neither to embody any worthy ideal
nor even to possess the merit of stability. In the
atmosphere of plain verity, where, as he said, "my
business is to teach my aspirations to conform themselves to fact, not to try and make facts harmonize with
my aspirations," he confidently looked for the hopes of
the future; but were it not so, he solemnly declared—

> If there is no hope of a large improvement of the
> condition of the greater part of the human family;
> if it is true that the increase of knowledge, the
> winning of a greater dominion over Nature which is
> its consequence, and the wealth which follows that
> dominion, are to make no difference in the extent
> and the intensity of want, with its concomitant
> physical and moral degradation among the masses of
> the people, I should hail the advent of some kindly
> comet which would sweep the whole affair away as
> a desirable consummation.

In the matter of personal conduct he rejected the
notions that the moral government of the world is imper-
fect without a system of future rewards and punishments,
and that such a system is indispensable to practical
morality. "I believe," he said, "that both these dogmas
are very mischievous lies."

There is no need for future compensation because, so
he firmly believed, "the Divine Government—if we may
use such a phrase to express the sum of the 'customs of
matter'—is wholly just......But for this to be clear we
must bear in mind what almost all forget, that the
rewards of life are contingent upon obedience to the
whole law—physical as well as moral—and that moral
obedience will not atone for physical sin, or *vice versâ*."
Thus he could declare "the more I know intimately of
the lives of other men (to say nothing of my own), the
more obvious it is that the wicked does *not* flourish, nor
is the righteous punished." "The gravitation of sin to

sorrow is as certain as that of the earth to the sun, and more so—for experimental proof of the fact is within reach of us all—nay, is before us all in our own lives, if we had but the eyes to see it."

Nevertheless—

It is to be recollected, in view of the apparent discrepancy between men's acts and their rewards, that Nature is juster than we are. She takes into account what a man brings with him into this world, which human justice cannot do. If I, born a bloodthirsty and savage brute, inheriting these qualities from others, kill you, my fellow-men will very justly hang me; but I shall not be visited with the horrible remorse which would be my real punishment if, my nature being higher, I had done the same thing.

Accordingly—

Not only do I disbelieve in the need for compensation, but I believe that the seeking for rewards and punishments out of this life leads men to a ruinous ignorance of the fact that their inevitable rewards and punishments are here.

If the expectation of hell hereafter can keep me from evil-doing, surely a fortiori the certainty of hell now will do so? If a man could be firmly impressed with the belief that stealing damaged him as much as swallowing arsenic would do (and it does), would not the dissuasive force of that belief be greater than that of any based on mere future expectations?

And this leads me to quote words written by an old friend and colleague of his, Sir Spencer Walpole :—

Of all the men I have ever known, his ideas and his standard were, on the whole, the highest. He recognized that the fact of his religious views imposed on him the duty of living the most upright of lives; and I am very much of the opinion of a little child, now grown into an accomplished woman,

who, when she was told that Professor Huxley had
no hope of future rewards and no fear of future
punishments, emphatically declared: " Then I think
Professor Huxley is the best man I have ever
known."

XIII

MORALITY AND THE CHURCH

IT is alike interesting and satisfactory to reflect that practical morality in civilized life is much the same for all earnest men, however they differ in their theories as to the origin of moral ideas and the kind of motives and sanctions to be insisted on for right action. It is true that the theologians and supernaturalists have erected their scaffolding around the building of social and human morality, vowing that it will not stand without. Yet it remains steady when the scaffolding is warped by the winds of doctrine or uprooted by advancing knowledge. The spirit that has built it is free from the perverted enthusiasms which crusade against freedom, put thought in fetters, and sanctify persecution. It lends no support to the other spirit that would dominate minds and consciences by formulæ that lie outside the court of reason. These things are of clericalism, and it was clericalism to which Huxley ever found himself in opposition, for it "raises obstacles to scientific ways of thinking, which are even more important than scientific discoveries." But all associations for promoting that sympathy which is at the foundation of human society need not be infected with clericalism. If such a step were otherwise expedient, even the State might do something towards that end indirectly :—

> I can conceive the existence of an Established Church which should be a blessing to the community. A Church in which, week by week, services should

be devoted, not to the iteration of abstract propositions in theology, but to the setting before men's
minds of an ideal of true, just, and pure living;
a place in which those who are weary of the burden
of daily cares should find a moment's rest in the
contemplation of the higher life which is possible
for all, though attained by so few ; a place in which
the man of strife and of business should have time
to think how small, after all, are the rewards he
covets compared with peace and charity. Depend
upon it, if such a Church existed, no one would seek
to disestablish it.

But, while sympathy is the basis of society and
enthusiasm the greatest motive power of humanity,
there remains something more to be considered. The
man who could appreciate the value of the personal
consolations brought by the Bible-woman to the poor and
down-trodden, and the infinitely comfortable assurance
of the mystic, firm as hypnotic conviction, that he is the
direct associate and instrument of the Almighty, whether
submissive or arrogant, from Stephen to the Bâb, from
Cromwell and Gordon to Bismarck and his Imperial
associates, such a man might well say : " I wish I could
be so magnificently self-confident, so untroubled by
doubt. But I can't, for I have to ask : Is it true ? ; and
I find that these persons base themselves upon very
questionable grounds."

True, that in regard to the place of good and evil in
this world the best theological teachers—

substantially recognize these realities of things,
however strange the forms in which they clothe
their conceptions. The doctrines of predestination,
of original sin, of the innate depravity of man and
the evil fate of the greater part of the race, of the
primacy of Satan in this world, of the essential
vileness of matter, of a malevolent Demiurgus
subordinate to a benevolent Almighty, who has only

lately revealed himself, faulty as they are, appear to
me to be vastly nearer the truth than the " liberal "
popular illusions that babies are all born good, and
that the example of a corrupt society is responsible
for their failure to remain so ; that it is given to
everybody to reach the ethical ideal if he will only
try ; that all partial evil is universal good, and other
optimistic figments, such as that which represents
" Providence " under the guise of a paternal philan-
thropist, and bids us believe that everything will
come right (according to our notions) at last.

......I am a very strong believer in the punishment
of certain kinds of actions, not only in the present,
but in all the future a man can have, be it long or
short.   Therefore in hell, for I suppose that all
men with a clear sense of right and wrong (and I
am not sure that any others deserve such punishment) have now and then " descended into hell "
and stopped there quite long enough to know what
infinite punishment means.   And if a genuine, not
merely subjective, immortality awaits us, I conceive
that, without some such change as that depicted in
the fifteenth chapter of *Corinthians*, immortality
must be eternal misery.   The fate of Swift's
Struldbrugs seems to me not more horrible than
that of a mind imprisoned for ever within the
flammantia moenia of inextinguishable memories.

Such were the shapes into which the Christian
theologians had fashioned a number of moral truths
when they annexed the house of human morality.   But
what is the basis of certitude on which these interpreta-
tions rest ?   If Adam was not an historical character, if
the story of the Fall be whittled down into a " type "
which is typical of no underlying reality, the basis of
Pauline theology is shaken, and practical deductions
drawn from it are shaken also.   In fact, " the Demonology of Christianity shows that its founders knew no
more about the spiritual world than anybody else, and

Newman's doctrine of 'Development' is true to an extent of which the Cardinal did not dream." And as to the argument that the successful spread of Christianity attests the truth of the New Testament story, he replied to his questioner with the general propositions :—

1. The Church founded by Jesus has *not* made its way; has *not* permeated the world; but *did* become extinct in the country of its birth—as Nazarenism and Ebionism.

2. The Church that did make its way and coalesced with the State in the fourth century had no more to do with the Church founded by Jesus than Ultramontanism has with Quakerism. It is Alexandrian Judaism and Neoplatonistic mystagogy, and as much of the old idolatry and demonology as could be got in under new or old names.

3. Paul has said that the Law was schoolmaster to Christ with more truth than he knew. Throughout the Empire the synagogues had their cloud of Gentile hangers-on—those who "feared God" and who were fully prepared to accept a Christianity which was merely an expurgated Judaism and the belief in Jesus as the Messiah.

4. The Christian "Sodalitia" were not merely religious bodies, but friendly societies, burial societies, and guilds. They hung together for all purposes; the mob hated them as it now hates the Jews in Eastern Europe, because they were more frugal, more industrious, and led better lives than their neighbours, while they stuck together like Scotchmen.

If these things are true—and I appeal to your knowledge of history that they are so—what has the success of Christianity to do with the truth or falsehood of the story of Jesus?

Furthermore, behind all the theological developments of the Church lies the whole question of Theism, and "the philosophical difficulties of Theism now are neither greater nor less than they have been ever since Theism was invented."

XIV

LIFE AND FRIENDSHIPS

"To live laborious days" was, for Huxley, at all times a necessity as well as a creed. The lover of knowledge and truth, he firmly believed, must devote his uttermost powers to their service; he held as strongly that every man's first duty to society was to support himself. But science provided more fame than pence, and with wife and family to support he was spurred to redoubled efforts. In the early years of married life especially, while he was still struggling to make his way, he often felt the pinch. He added to his modest income by reviewing and translating scientific books and by lecturing. On one occasion, when he was a candidate for a certain scientific lectureship, one of the committee of election, a wealthy man, expressed astonishment at his application—"what can he want with a hundred a year?" "I dare say," commented Huxley, "he pays his cook that." In early days, visioning the future, he and his wife had fondly planned to marry on £400 a year, while he pursued science, unknown if need be, for the sake of science. The reality pressed hardly upon them; those were dark evenings when he would come home fagged out by a second lecture at the end of a full day's work and lay himself down wearily on one couch, while she, so long a semi-invalid, lay uselessly on another. And, later, the upbringing of a large family, though its advent made life the more worth living, involved a heavy strain. At the same time, a man who was ever ready to take up responsibilities for the furtherance of every branch of science with which he was concerned had endless responsibilities committed to him. Besides his researches in pure science, whether anatomy, paleontology, or anthropology, his regular teaching work and other courses of lectures, his long work as examiner at the London University, the production of scientific memoirs and text-books and more general essays, he took a leading share in editing the *Natural History Review* for two and a-half years; he was an active supporter of the chief scientific societies to which he belonged, and took a prominent part in their administration as member of council, secretary, or president, the most laborious period of which was during the nine years of his secretaryship of the Royal Society, soon to be followed by the presidency. Add to these his service on the School Board and no less than eight Royal Commissions, and it is easy to see that the longest working days he could contrive were always filled and over-filled.

When very tired he would occasionally dash off for a week or two's walking with a friend in Wales, or some corner of France; two summer holidays in Switzerland with John Tyndall resulted in a joint paper on the "Structure of Glacier Ice"; later, the family holidays by the sea regularly saw a good deal of time devoted to writing, while his exercise consisted of long walks.

Unlike Darwin, who at last found nothing save science engrossing enough to make him oblivious of his constant ill-health, Huxley never lost his keen delight in literature and art. He was a rapid and omnivorous reader, devouring everything from a fairy tale to a blue book, and tearing the heart out of a book at express speed. With this went a love of great and beautiful poetry and of prose expression that is at once exact and artistically balanced. "I have a great love and respect for my native tongue," he wrote, "and take great pains to use it properly. Sometimes I write essays half-a-dozen times before I can get them into the proper shape ; and I believe I become more fastidious as I grow older." Indeed, even after much re-writing, his corrections in proof must have appalled his publishers. "Science and literature," he declared, "are not two things, but two sides of one thing." "Have something to say, and say it," was the great Duke's theory of style. "Say it in such language," added Huxley, "that you can stand cross-examination on every word. Be clear, though you may be convicted of error. If you are clearly wrong, you will run up against a fact some time and get set right. If you shuffle with your subject, and study chiefly to use language which will give a loophole of escape either way, there is no hope for you."

Herein lay the secret of his lucidity. Uniting the scientific habit of mind with the literary art, he showed that truthfulness need not be bald, and that power lies rather in accuracy than in luxuriance of diction. As to the influence which such a style exerted on the habit of mind of his readers, there is remarkable testimony in a letter from Spedding, the editor of Bacon, printed in the Life of Huxley, ii, 239. Spedding, his senior by a score of years, describes the influence of Bacon on his own style in the matter of exactitude, the pruning of fine epithets and sweeping statements, the reduction of numberless superlatives to positives, and asserts that if, as a young man, he had fallen in with Huxley's writings before Bacon's, they would have produced the same effect upon him.

Huxley's own criticism of the one and only poem he ever published is also instructive. On his way back from the funeral of Tennyson in Westminster Abbey, he spent the journey in shaping out some lines on the dead poet, the germ of which had come into his mind in the Abbey. These, with a number of other tributes to Tennyson by professed poets, were printed in the *Nineteenth Century* for November, 1892. He writes in a private letter :—

> If I were to pass judgment upon it in comparison with the others, I should say that as to style it is hammered, and as to feeling, human.
>
> They are castings of much prettier pattern and of mainly poetico-classical educated-class sentiment. I do not think there is a line of mine one of my old working-class audience would have boggled over.

As regards the arts other than literary, he had a keen eye for a picture or a piece of sculpture, for, in addition to the draughtman's and anatomist's sense of form, he had a strong sense of colour. To good music, also, he was always susceptible ; as a young man he used to sing a little, but his voice, though true, was never strong. In music, as in painting, he was untrained. Yet, as has been noted already, his illustrations to MacGillivray's *Voyage of the Rattlesnake* and his holiday sketches suggest that he might have gone far had he been trained as an artist.

When first married he used to set aside Saturday afternoons to take his wife to the Ella concerts, fore-runners of the " Saturday Pops.," but it was not very long before the pressure of circumstance forbade this pleasure. Later, he very occasionally managed to go to the theatre ; but his chief recreation, apart from change of work and the rapid devouring of a good novel, was in meeting his friends, when occasion offered, at the scientific societies or at dinner, or now and then in country visits which had not yet received the name of " week-ends."

When, in the middle seventies, his position was firmly established and he was living in a roomy house, No. 4 Marlborough Place, St. John's Wood, there were gatherings of friends on Sunday evenings. An informal meal awaited the guests, who came either on a general invitation or when specially bidden ; others put in an appearance later. There would be much talk, from grave to gay, in those plainly appointed rooms, or on a fine summer evening, perhaps, in the garden with its little lawn behind the house. Some music, too, was almost sure to be performed by friends or by the daughters of the house, whose progress in the art of singing was ever a matter of concern to Mr. Herbert Spencer, himself a great lover of music. Letters and Art were well represented there as well as Science, intermingled with the friends of the younger generation. " Here," writes G. W. Smalley,

> people from many other worlds than those of abstract science were bidden ; where talk was to be heard of a kind rare in any world. It was scientific at times, but subdued to the necessities of the occasion ; speculative, yet kept within such bounds that bishop or archbishop might have listened without offence ; political even, and still not commonplace, and, when artistic, free from affectation.
>
> There and elsewhere Mr. Huxley easily took the lead if he cared to, or if challenged. Nobody was more ready in a greater variety of topics, and if they were scientific it was almost always another who introduced them. Unlike some of his comrades of the Royal Society, he was of opinion that man does not live by science alone, and nothing came amiss to him......Even in private the alarm of war is sometimes heard, and Mr. Huxley is not a whit less formidable as a disputant across the table than with pen in hand. Yet an angry man must be very angry indeed before he could be angry with this adversary. He disarmed his enemies with an amiable grace that made defeat endurable, if not entirely delightful.

If scientific subjects came up in conversation, the luminous style, so familiar in his written work, reappeared in talk.

> Yet it has more than that. You cannot listen to him without thinking more of the speaker than of his science, more of the solid beautiful nature than of the intellectual gifts, more of his manly simplicity and sincerity than of all his knowledge and his long services.

But in the intermediate period, from about 1860 onwards, the unceasing rush of occupation rendered it very difficult to keep in touch with his friends. On his initiative a small dining club of scientific friends and allies was established. Almost all these close friends were members of the Royal Society, and were likely to attend its meetings. Dinner, therefore, was to be taken at a convenient hotel before the monthly meeting of the Society, and those who were inevitably drifting apart under the stress of circumstances would have a regular meeting ground. This was the famous x Club, a name singularly appropriate on the principle of *lucus a non lucendo* to a club of nine members who never proceeded to the election of a tenth. Opinions as to the name and constitution of the little society being no less numerous than the members—indeed more so—"we finally accepted the happy suggestion of our mathematicians to call it the x Club ; and the proposal of some genius among us that we should have no rules, save the unwritten law not to have any, was carried by acclamation."

Huxley first propounded the scheme to his most intimate friends, Joseph Dalton Hooker, then Assistant Director of Kew, and John Tyndall, Professor of Natural Philosophy at the Royal Institution. George Busk, the anatomist, afterwards President of the College of Surgeons, was another whose friendship dated from soon after the

G

return of the *Rattlesnake* to England. Herbert Spencer, the philosopher, and Sir John Lubbock, banker and naturalist, were friends of nearly as long standing. Edward Frankland, Professor of Chemistry at the Royal Institution, and Thomas Archer Hirst, Professor of Physics and Pure Mathematics at University College, London, afterwards Director of Naval Studies at the Royal Naval College, Greenwich, entered the circle as special friends of Tyndall's. William Spottiswoode, Queen's Printer and mathematician, was the ninth member, elected by the rest at the first meeting.

Between them they could have managed to contribute most of the articles to a scientific Encyclopædia : six were Presidents of the British Association ; three were Associates of the Institute of France ; and from among them the Royal Society chose a Secretary, a Foreign Secretary, a Treasurer, and three successive Presidents. Meeting though they did for the sake of friendship and good fellowship, it was inevitable that they should discuss the burning questions of the scientific world freely from varied points of view, and, being all animated by similar ideas of the high function of science and of the great Society, the chief representative of science to which all but one of them belonged, they incidentally exercised a strong influence on the progress of scientific organization.

The first meeting took place on November 3, 1864 ; nearly nineteen years passed before the circle was broken by the death of Spottiswoode. Proposals were made to fill the gap with a new friend, but, as the *raison d'être* of the club had been simply the personal attachment of the original nine, the project fell through. Finally, after Hirst's death in 1892, when five out of the remaining six were living away from London and for the most part in uncertain health, it became more and more difficult to arrange a meeting, and the club quietly lapsed after nearly twenty-eight years of existence.

Guests were often entertained at the x dinners, men of science or letters of almost every nationality—a delightful and quite informal mode of personal intercourse. In the summer, also, the x often made a weekend expedition into the country or up the river, in which the wives of the married members took part, the formula for the invitation being $x's + yv's$.

XV

CHARLES DARWIN

To this focus of close friendships Charles Darwin would assuredly have been invited to belong had he been other than an invalid living away from London; for he was the warm and revered friend not only of Huxley, but still more of Hooker, who in age stood midway between the two —eight years younger than the one and eight years older than the other—and who, for some fifteen years before the publication of the *Origin of Species*, had been Darwin's most intimate friend and aid in his work.

Huxley had made Darwin's acquaintance early in the fifties, and soon fell under the spell of his deep thought, his utter sincerity and generous warmth of heart. Darwin, for his part, was strongly attracted by his new friend's penetrating knowledge, incisive criticism, and brilliant conversation. When, in 1858, he began to write out the *Origin*, Huxley was one of the three men he fixed upon by whose judgment of the book he meant to abide. Lyell, who had read the book before it came out, was the first; Hooker, his long-time aid and critic and finally convert, the second. On the eve of publication, secure of these, he adds: "If I can convert Huxley I shall be content."

On all three the effect of the completed book, with its array of detailed argument and evidence, was far greater than that of previous discussions. With one or two reservations as to the logical completeness of the theory, Huxley accepted it as a well-founded working hypothesis, calculated to explain problems otherwise inexplicable.

There were evolutionists before Darwin, from Lamarck and the author of the *Vestiges of Creation* to Herbert Spencer; but as there was no evidence to bear out the orthodox creational view of the Book of *Genesis*, enlarged upon in detail by Milton, so before Darwin the evidence in favour of the transmutation of species was wholly insufficient, and no suggestion which had been made to the causes of the assumed transmutation was in any way adequate to explain the phenomena. Under such conditions only an agnostic attitude was possible. " So," writes Huxley—

> I took refuge in that *"thätige Skepsis,"* which Goethe has so well defined, and, reversing the apostolic precept to be all things to all men, I usually defended the tenability of the received doctrines when I had to do with the transmutationists, and stood up for the possibility of transmutation among the orthodox, thereby, no doubt, increasing an already current, but quite undeserved, reputation for needless combativeness.

Then came the publication of the Darwin-Wallace paper in 1858, and of the *Origin* in 1859, the effect of which he compares to—

> the flash of light which, to a man who has lost himself on a dark night, suddenly reveals a road which, whether it takes him straight home or not, certainly goes his way. That which we were looking for, and could not find, was an hypothesis respecting the origin of known organic forms which assumed the operation of no causes but such as could be proved to be actually at work. We wanted, not to pin our faith to that or any other speculation, but to get hold of clear and definite conceptions which could be brought face to face with facts and have their validity tested. The *Origin* provided us with the working hypothesis we sought. Moreover, it did the immense service of freeing us for ever

from the dilemma—refuse to accept the creation
hypothesis and what have you to propose that can
be accepted by any cautious reasoner? In 1857 I
had no answer ready, and I do not think that any
one else had. A year later we reproached ourselves
with dullness for being perplexed with such an
inquiry. My reflection, when I first made myself
master of the central idea of the *Origin*, was : " How
extremely stupid not to have thought of that." I
suppose that Columbus's companions said much the
same when he made the egg stand on end. The
facts of variability, of the struggle for existence, of
adaptation to conditions, were notorious enough ;
but none of us had suspected that the road to the
heart of the species problem lay through them until
Darwin and Wallace dispelled the darkness, and the
beacon-fire of the *Origin* guided the benighted.

Whether the particular shape which the doctrine
of Evolution, as applied to the organic world, took in
Darwin's hands would prove to be final or not, was
to me a matter of indifference. In my earliest
criticisms of the *Origin* I ventured to point out that
its logical foundation was insecure so long as experiments in selective breeding had not produced
varieties which were more or less infertile ; and that
insecurity remains up to the present time. But,
with any and every critical doubt which my sceptical
ingenuity could suggest, the Darwinian hypothesis
remained incomparably more probable than the
creation hypothesis. And if we had none of us been
able to discern the paramount significance of some
of the most patent and notorious of natural facts,
until they were, so to speak, thrust under our noses,
what force remained in the dilemma—creation or
nothing? It was obvious that hereafter the proba-
bility would be immensely greater, that the links of
natural causation were hidden from our purblind
eyes, than that natural causation should be incompetent to produce all the phenomena of nature. The
only rational course for those who had no other

object than the attainment of truth was to accept "Darwinism" as a working hypothesis and see what could be made of it. Either it would prove its capacity to elucidate the facts of organic life or it would break down under the strain. This was surely the dictate of common sense, and for once common sense carried the day.

Mention has been made of the instant support he was able to lend the *Origin* in the *Times* review of the book, and the extension of its doctrines in regard to man. Even before the book appeared, however, he began to act as what Darwin laughingly called his "general agent." His address on "Persistent Types" (June, 1859) aimed at clearing up in advance one of the obvious objections raised against acceptance of the doctrine of Evolution—namely, how is it that, if evolution is ever progressive, progress is not universal? How is it that all forms do not necessarily advance, and that simple organisms still exist? As it happened, Darwin did not discuss this point when he first put the *Origin* together, and speedily came to regard this as the most serious omission in the book.

Great, then, was the debt of all science to Darwin. And not of science only. The fight for freedom of thought and speech in science, into which Huxley especially threw himself, was the more successful because the immediate cause he upheld was so overwhelmingly strong in reason and demonstration; and, the supreme curb upon thought being once broken, a wider freedom was gained.

For Darwin, therefore, Huxley had the reverence due to one who had forged a new and mighty weapon in the war for plain truth. But, while he could not but uphold a theory so much in accord with his own knowledge and so fruitful in its promise of new knowledge, whether the author of it were his friend or not, admiration and affection for a man of such utter sincerity, such selfless respect for truth, and warm personality, led him, when those views were stupidly or maliciously attacked, to take more trouble in his defence and support, and to strike out much harder at his adversary than he would otherwise have done. Darwin's friends were well assured that the scanty time which his health allowed for work was far too precious to be wasted in controversy; for his own sake and for the sake of the calm atmosphere in which a great theory should be worked out, they thought that the battling on a lower plane should be left to them. " You ought to be like one of the blessed gods of Elysium, and let the inferior deities do battle with the infernal powers." " If I say a savage thing," Huxley told him, " it is only ' pretty Fanny's way '; but if you do, it is not likely to be forgotten." Hence a dash of personal pleasure was infused into the duty of upholding and defending the bringer of new light.

The acquaintance had begun about 1851; there was a common bond in their sea experiences and explorations, as well as in their search after a wider philosophy, to include the teachings of natural science; the older man found in the younger a source of much biological and other information, a suggestive critic and a stimulating companion. Their relations took a long step towards intimacy after 1861, when, after the loss of her eldest child, Mrs. Huxley and her other children made a long stay at Down, and entered upon a life-long friendship with Mrs. Darwin and the family. Thereafter followed many visits to Down, and, whenever Darwin was in London, the certainty of half-an-hour's keen talk—all that the doctor allowed—with his friend and fellow-worker on some critical question of the moment.

Darwin's admiration of his friend's powers was outspoken. To quote one or two expressions of it: Huxley had delivered, in 1862, six lectures to working men, which were printed off each week as delivered in "little green pamphlets," under the general title of "On Our Knowledge of the Causes of the Phenomena of Organic Nature," winding up with an account of the bearing of the *Origin* upon the complete theory of these causes. Acknowledging Nos. IV and V, Darwin writes :—

They are simply perfect. They ought to be largely advertised ; but it is very good in me to say so, for I threw down No. IV with this reflection: "What is the good of me writing a thundering big book when everything is in this green little book, so despicable for its size?" In the name of all that is good and bad, I may as well shut up shop altogether.

After reading the article "Mr. Darwin's Critics" in 1871, he wrote yet more enthusiastically. Mr. Mivart, in an apologia for the attitude of Roman Catholicism towards Evolution, twitted the generality of men of science with their ignorance of the real doctrines of his Church, and cited the Jesuit theologian, Suarez, the latest great representative of scholasticism, as following St. Augustine in asserting derivative creation—that is, evolution from primordial matter endowed with certain powers. Huxley thereupon examined the works of the learned Jesuit, and found not only that the particular reference was not to the point, but that, in his tract on the "Six Days of Creation," Suarez expressly rejects the doctrine and reprehends Augustine for holding it. "So," write Huxley gleefully at the irony of the situation, "I have come out in the new character of a defender of Catholic orthodoxy, and upset Mivart out of the mouth of his own prophet."

In the course of a most appreciative letter Darwin exclaimed :—

What a wonderful man you are to grapple with

those old metaphysico-divinity books......The pendulum is now swinging against our side, but I feel positive it will soon swing the other way; and no mortal man will do half as much as you in giving it a start in the right dire ion, as you did at the commencement.

And then, after "mounting climax on climax," he adds: "I must tell you what Hooker said to me a few years ago. 'When I read Huxley I feel quite infantile in intellect.'"

The most touching act of friendship, and one which assuredly gave personal point to Huxley's remark in another connection, "Darwin is in all things noble and generous—one of those people who think it a privilege to let him help," took place when Huxley's health had utterly broken down in 1873, and he was as depressed in mind as in body. Who could say No to these words from the oldest and most venerated among his devoted friends?—

Down, Beckenham, Kent.
April 23, 1873.

My dear Huxley,

I have been asked by some of your friends (eighteen in number) to inform you that they have placed through Robarts, Lubbock, and Company the sum of £2,100 to your account at your bankers. We have done this to enable you to get such complete rest as you may require for the re-establishment of your health; and in doing this we are convinced that we act for the public interest, as well as in accordance with our most earnest desires. Let me assure you that we are all your warm personal friends, and that there is not a stranger or mere acquaintance among us. If you could have heard what was said, or could have read what was, as I believe, our inmost thoughts, you would know that we all feel towards you as we should to an honoured and much-loved brother. I am sure that you will return this feeling, and will therefore be glad to give us the opportunity of aiding you in some degree, as this will be a happiness to us to the last day of our lives. Let me add that our plan occurred to several of your friends at nearly the same time, and quite independently of one another.

My dear Huxley, your affectionate friend,

CHARLES DARWIN.

Huxley was deeply moved. "What have I done to deserve this?" he exclaimed. Before this generosity he at last allowed himself to confess that, in the long struggle against ill health, he had been beaten; but, as he said, only enough to teach him humility.

The relief from anxieties, the ultimate restoration to health through a clear holiday, were an unforgettable gift from this "band of brothers," and the sufferer who had been healed rejoiced when not long after an opportunity arose to share in a similar gift of help and healing to another of the same good fellowship.

XVI

HOOKER, FORBES, TYNDALL, AND SPENCER

OF his nearer contemporaries the two most intimate and faithful of his life-long friendships were with Tyndall and Hooker, concerning the utter frankness of which he writes to the latter :—

> I wish you wouldn't be apologetic about criticism from people who have a right to criticize. I always look upon any criticism as a compliment, not but what the old Adam in T. H. H. *will* arise and fight vigorously against all impugnment and irrespective of all odds in the way of authority, but that is the way of the beast. Why I value your and Tyndall's and Darwin's friendship so much is, among other things, that you all pitch into me when necessary. You may depend upon it, however blue I may look when in the wrong, it's wrath with myself and nobody else.

The common note in these friendships was not only community of aims, but an essential generosity and sincerity. This it was that had drawn him so strongly to Edward Forbes among the leaders of biology when he returned, an unknown but promising pioneer of science, from the voyage of the *Rattlesnake*. For Forbes inspired his admiration and affection as a man of letters and an artist who had not merged the *man* in the man of science ; free from pedantry or jealousy—the two besetting faults of literary and scientific men ; earnest, disinterested, ready to give his time and influence to help any man who was working for the cause ; one of the few to whom

1

a proud man could feel obliged without losing a particle of independence or self-respect.

> My notions [he writes] are diametrically opposed to his in some matters, and he helps me to oppose him......I had a long paper read at the Royal Society which opposed some of his views, and he got up and spoke in the highest terms of it afterwards. This is all as it should be. I can reverence such a man and yet respect myself.

Without his aid and sympathy the young man would never have persevered in the course he ventured to choose, and in following which it was one of his greatest hopes that they should work in harmony for long years at the aims so dear to both.

"One could trust him so thoroughly!" There lay the root of friendship. And the trust was thoroughly reciprocated. The entire frankness between friends is brightly illustrated by the history of the award of the Royal Medal in 1854. As a member of the Royal Society Council, Huxley had to vote on the names proposed for the various medals. For the Royal Medal first Hooker was named, and received his hearty support; then Forbes was put up, in his eyes equally deserving, and almost more closely bound to him by ties of active friendship, so that, whichever way he ultimately voted, his action might possibly be ascribed to personal, not scientific, motives. Thereupon he explained to the Council that he considered their claims equal; that, whichever chanced to have been put forward first, he would never have proposed the other in opposition to him. As he had spoken of Hooker's merits, so also he spoke of Forbes's, positively, and not by way of comparison; and this done, voted for both!

Hooker was actually elected. Huxley then wrote to both his friends, explaining fully what he had done.

Had he felt that one of the two had strongly superior claims, and thought it right to vote for him only, the other, he was sure, would have fully appreciated his motives, and it would have done no injury to their friendship.

He was not mistaken.   Among his most precious possessions he kept Forbes's reply :—

> I heartily concur in the course you have taken, and, had I been placed as you have been, would have done exactly the same......Your way of proceeding was as true an act of friendship as any that could be performed.   As to myself, I dream so little about medals that the notion of being on the list never entered my brain, even when asleep.   If it ever comes, I shall be pleased and thankful ; if it does not, it is not the sort of thing to break my equanimity.   Indeed, I would always like to see it given not as a mere honour, but as a help to a good man, and this it is assuredly in Hooker's case. Government people are so ignorant that they require to have people's merits drummed into their heads by all possible means, and Hooker's getting the medal may be of real service to him before long.   I am in a snug, though not an idle, nest ; he has not got his resting-place yet.   And so, my dear Huxley, I trust that you know me too well to think that I am either grieved or envious ; and you, Hooker, and I are much of the same way of thinking.

Frankness was the only remedy for such an imbroglio, and, as Huxley wrote to Hooker about a similar case a couple of years later :—

> It's deuced hard to keep straight in this wicked world, but, as you say, the only chance is to out with it, and I thank you much for writing so frankly about the matter.

With Hooker, the keen observer and critical reasoner, the man of warm impulses and sane judgments, he had

From a Photograph by Downey, 1890

To face p. 102

a peculiarly intimate bond of friendship summed up in a
letter of 1888, when they had received the Copley medal
in successive years :—

> It is very pleasant to have our niches in the
> Pantheon close together. It is getting on for forty
> years since we were first " acquent," and, considering
> with what a very considerable dose of tenacity,
> vivacity, and that glorious firmness (which the
> beasts who don't like us call obstinacy) we are
> both endowed, the fact that we have never had the
> shadow of a shade of a quarrel is more to our credit
> than being ex-Presidents and Copley medallists.
> But we have had a masonic bond in both being
> well salted in early life. I have always felt that
> I owed a great deal to my acquaintance with the
> realities of things gained in the old *Rattlesnake*.

From earliest days, soon after they had returned, the
one from the South Seas, the other from the Himalayas,
they had stood shoulder to shoulder confidently in the
struggle to put science on a firm and independent footing.
When the future of the Natural History Collections at
the British Museum was in the balance, they energetically
resolved to constitute themselves into a permanent "Committee of Safety," to watch over what was being done
and take measures with the advice of others when necessary. Together as biologists they realized the greatness
of Darwin's vision ; together they bore the brunt of the
battle of the *Origin* at Oxford. In seeking a good
mouthpiece for scientific opinion, in reorganizing and
administering the great scientific societies, in their work
for scientific education, they shared the same ideas, and
their friendship and Tyndall's formed the starting-point
of the *x* Club, with its regular meetings of old friends.
More than once they went off on a short holiday tour
together, and when Huxley was invalided in 1873 it
was Hooker who took charge and carried him off for a

month's active trip in the geological paradise of the
Auvergne. The care and company of so good a friend
made the crowning ingredient in a most successful
prescription. And when both had retired from official
life a new interest in common sprang up through
Huxley's incursion into botany. While recruiting his
health in the high Alps, his interest was aroused by
the Gentians, and he wrote a valuable paper on their
morphology and distribution. This interest continued
itself into the making of a rock-garden in his Eastbourne
home, where, in his spare hours, he proceeded to put
into happy practice Candide's famous maxim, " *Cultivons
notre jardin*," and drew from this occupation the simile
of the wild chalk down and the cultivated garden in his
Romanes Lecture to illustrate the contrast between the
cosmic process and the social organism.

Hooker often sent his friend plants from his own
garden, sometimes banteringly including one which would
" flourish in any neglected corner."

An unclouded intimacy of friendship lasted to the end,
and it was Hooker who received the last letter written
by his friend.

Close as a brother, too, and claiming the name of
brother in affectionate adoption, was John Tyndall,
radiant in genial warmth and high spirits. They, too,
were at one in thoughts, sympathies, and aims ; they
travelled together, especially in the Alps, where Tyndall
mainly carried out the investigation of certain problems
in relation to the glaciers which Huxley had suggested
to him, and, being " a masterful man and over-generous,"
insisted that the resulting paper on glaciers should bear
both their names.

Tyndall came to the School of Mines as Professor of
Physics in 1859 at his friend's instigation, and for nine
years they were, as colleagues, in daily contact, and

indeed were not far separated when Tyndall succeeded Faraday at the Royal Institution in Albemarle Street.

Tyndall, who remained a bachelor till late in middle life, always found a warm corner beside his friend's hearth. From the earliest days of the household in the little house at Waverley Place he was admitted to the inner circle of a lively friendship by Mrs. Huxley also, that keen judge of character, and to the children ranked as a kind of unofficial uncle. On New Year's Day he was chief among the two or three intimates who were bidden here, having no domestic hearth of their own, Herbert Spencer and Hirst being the other "regulars," and later Michael Foster.

As the two men both had ready pens and stood side by side in many controversies, they came to be regarded by the public as a pair of Great Twin Brethren, the Castor and Pollux of many a scientific battle of Lake Regillus. Odd confusions sometimes followed. In 1876, not long after Tyndall's marriage to the daughter of Lord Claud Hamilton, Huxley was described in a newspaper paragraph as setting out for America "with his titled bride," and even, on Tyndall's death, received the doubtful honour of a funeral sermon.

True that they did not see eye to eye on some of the most fundamental matters of social and political principle, and where they did Tyndall's vehement enthusiasm would sometimes sweep him into activities where his friend could not follow. But these things were no bar to their mutual affection and esteem, and in token of this two letters of 1866 may be quoted, when England was sharply divided on the question of Governor Eyre's action in suppressing an incipient revolt in Jamaica.

In particular, a negro preacher named Gordon had been arrested, court-martialled, and summarily executed. A Royal Commission appointed to inquire into the case

H

declared that the evidence given appeared to be wholly
insufficient to establish the charge upon which the
prisoner took his trial, and that in the evidence adduced
they could not see any sufficient proof of Gordon's
complicity in the outbreak, or of having been a party to
any general conspiracy against the Government.

To many thoughtful and law-abiding persons such
a proceeding appeared to be no better than judicial
murder, constituting a hideous precedent ; a committee
was formed to present a formal indictment against
Governor Eyre and obtain a judicial pronouncement on
the question, quite apart from the two other questions
persistently confused with it—namely, was Gordon
a Jamaica Hampden or was he a psalm-singing firebrand,
and was Governor Eyre actuated by the highest and
noblest motives, or was he under the influence of panic-
stricken rashness or worse impulses ?

With this high constitutional end in view—the protec-
tion of individual liberty—Huxley joined the committee.
To Charles Kingsley, who confessed to taking the hero-
worshipper's view of Governor Eyre, Huxley replied :—

I dare say he did all this with the best of motives
and in a heroic vein. But if English law will not
declare that heroes have no more right to kill people
in this fashion than other folk, I shall take an early
opportunity of migrating to Texas or some other
quiet place where there is less hero-worship and
more respect for justice, which is to my mind of
much more importance than hero-worship.

In point of fact, men take sides on this question,
not so much by looking at the mere facts of the
case, but rather as their deepest political convictions
lead them. And the great use of the prosecution,
and one of my reasons for joining it, is that it will
help a great many people to find out what their
profoundest political beliefs are.

The hero-worshippers who believe that the world

is to be governed by its great men, who are to lead
the little ones, justly if they can, but, if not, unjustly
drive or kick them the right way, will sympathize
with Mr. Eyre.

The other sect (to which I belong), who look upon
hero-worship as no better than any other idolatry
and upon the attitude of mind of the hero-worshipper
as essentially immoral ; who think it is better for
a man to go wrong in freedom than to go right in
chains ; who look upon the observance of inflexible
justice as between man and man as of far greater
importance than even the preservation of social
order, will believe that Mr. Eyre has committed one
of the greatest crimes of which a person in authority
can be guilty, and will strain every nerve to obtain
a declaration that their belief is in accordance with
the law of England.

People who differ on fundamentals are not likely
to convert one another. To you, as to my dear
friend Tyndall, with whom I almost always act, but
who in this matter is as much opposed to me as you
are, I can only say, let us be strong enough and
wise enough to fight the question out as a matter of
principle and without bitterness.

To Tyndall, whose convictions were bred in Ulster and
fostered by an ardent devotion to Carlyle, he wrote in
the same strain, apropos of a friend's banter on their
sudden division :—

I replied to the jest earnestly enough—that I
hoped and believed our old friendship was strong
enough to stand any strain that might be put on it,
much as I grieved that we should be ranged in
opposite camps in this or any other case.

That you and I have fundamentally different
political principles must, I think, have become
obvious to both of us during the progress of the
American War. The fact is made still more plain
by your printed letter, the tone and spirit of which
I greatly admire, without being able to recognize in

it any important fact or argument which had not passed through my mind before I joined the Jamaica Committee.

Thus there is nothing for it but for us to agree to differ, each supporting his own side to the best of his ability and respecting his friend's freedom as he would his own, and doing his best to remove all petty bitterness from that which is at bottom one of the most important constitutional battles in which Englishmen have for many years been engaged.

If you and I are strong enough and wise enough, we shall be able to do this, and yet preserve that love for one another which I value as one of the good things of my life.

That public controversy could be conducted without loss of friendship he showed also in debate with Herbert Spencer. Their private encounters in argument were often very lively, for Spencer was a most tenacious disputant, to whom argument was as the breath of life.

It was probably after a meeting of the *x* Club, in the freedom of which debate was likely to be of the liveliest, that Spencer wrote accusing himself of losing his temper, and received the following reply :—

Your conscience has been treating you with the most extreme and unjust severity.

I recollect you *looked* rather savage at one point in our discussion, but I do assure you that you committed no overt act of ferocity ; and if you had, I think I should have fully deserved it for joining in the ferocious onslaught we all made upon you.

What your sins may be in this line to other folk I don't know, but, so far as I am concerned, I assure you I have often said that I know no one who takes aggravated opposition better than yourself, and that I have not a few times been ashamed of the extent to which I have tried your patience.

So you see that you have what the Buddhists call a stock of accumulated merit, *envers moi* ; and if

you should ever feel inclined to "d— my eyes,"
you can do so and have a balance left.

Seriously, my old friend, you must not think it
necessary to apologize to me about any such matters,
but believe me (d—ned or und—d),—Ever yours
faithfully......

If he was comrade and brother among the friends of
his own generation, he was a living inspiration to the
friends of the next generation, especially to the pupils
and teaching lieutenants who worked in close touch with
him. His younger disciples always felt that in acute
criticism and vast learning nobody surpassed him ; but
what they yet more admired than his learning was his
wisdom. It was a delight to read an essay fresh from
his pen, but an ever so much higher delight to hear him
talk for five minutes. "His," says Professor Hubrecht,
"was the most beautiful and the most manly intellect
I ever knew of." The personal affection as well as
admiration he inspired may be gathered from Sir E. Ray
Lankester's words : "There has been no man or woman
whom I have met in my journey through life whom
I have loved and regarded as I have him, and I feel that
the world has shrunk and become a poor thing now that
his splendid spirit and delightful presence are gone
from it." And Professor Jeffery Parker concludes his
Recollections of his old chief with these words :—

Whether a professor is usually a hero to his
demonstrator I cannot say ; I only know that,
looking back across an interval of many years and a
distance of half the circumference of the globe, I
have never ceased to be impressed with the manli-
ness and sincerity of his character, his complete
honesty of purpose, his high moral standard, his
scorn of everything mean or shifty, his firm deter-
mination to speak what he held to be truth at whatever cost of popularity. And for these things "I

loved the man, and do honour to his memory, on this side idolatry, as much as any."

Indeed, his relations with his demonstrators were typical of his judgment of men, his distinction between the essential and the unessential, which made him a successful administrator.

To a new subordinate " The General," as he was always called, was rather stern and exacting; but when once he was convinced that his man was to be trusted, he practically let him take his own course ; never interfered in matters of detail, accepted suggestions with the greatest courtesy and good humour, and was always ready with a kindly and humorous word of encouragement in times of difficulty. I was once grumbling to him about how hard it was to carry on the work of the laboratory through a long series of November fogs, " when neither sun nor stars in many days appeared." " Never mind, Parker," he said, instantly capping my quotation, " cast four anchors out of the stern and wish for day."

The first passport to his friendship was entire sincerity. Whatever other claims might be advanced, he would shut out from any approach to intimacy those whom he found to be untruthful or not straightforward. Naturally he did not offer any unnecessary encouragement to bores and dullards, but in his intercourse with these undesirables and wasters of his time he adopted none of the " offensive-defensive " methods of, say, Dr. Johnson or Lord Westbury. He armed himself with a cold correctitude of politeness, and lowered the social temperature instead of raising it.

XVII

IN THE FAMILY CIRCLE

His acquaintance and friendship were eagerly sought, and to those who entered the circle he gave abundantly of his brilliant gifts and of friendly affection; but the inmost circle was small—the men who were comrades and brothers; the sister and the brother united with him in love and trust; the wife to win whom he served so long, and without whose sustaining help and comradeship his quick spirit and nervous temperament could hardly have endured the long and often embittered struggle.

In this inmost circle he was at once strong and tender. The friend who most cordially admired his intellectual vigour and unflinching honesty could write after his death that—

> what now dwells most in my mind is the memory of old kindness, and of the days when I used to see him with (his wife) and his children. I may safely say that I never came from your house without thinking how good he is; what a tender and affectionate nature the man has. It did me good simply to see him.

Always the home was the inmost centre of his own life. Here he found personal solace in his long struggle; the sympathy that was the pillar and stay of his genius, the twin incentive to labour and achievement, the warmth that gave a fuller value to the light he ensued. None knew more perfectly than himself what he owed to his life-long companion, who, in turn, was as much uplifted by his eager spirit as she was proud to be the cherisher

111

of his aspirations and the active minister to his attainment. To her critical ear he gave the first reading of his essays ; the judgment and the praise that he most valued were hers, and, as he put it towards the end of his life, when he was travelling with his son in Madeira and had been cut off from letters longer than he liked :—

> Catch me going out of reach of letters again. I have been horridly anxious. Nobody—children or any one else—can be to me what you are. Ulysses preferred his old woman to immortality, and this absence has led me to see that he was as wise in that as in other things.

Quick and keen-edged as he was, I cannot recall his ever losing his temper with any of us at home. Firm he was under his great tenderness for children ; those nearest him felt a certain awe before the infallible force of his moral judgments ; his arbitrament, though rarely invoked, was instant and final. Going out into the world afterwards, I think we did not fail to realize how different the home atmosphere must be where self-control does not rule, and the inevitable rubs of life find vent in irritable and ill-considered words.

It was one of the penalties of his hard-driven existence that for the first fifteen or twenty years of his married life he had scarcely any time to devote to his children. The "lodger," as he used to describe himself, who went out early and came back late, could sometimes spare half-an-hour just before or just after dinner to draw wonderful pictures for the little ones, or on a Sunday he would now and then walk with the elder ones to Hampstead Heath or to the Zoo, where, as a constant visitant to the prosector's laboratory, he was a well-known figure, and admitted by the keepers to their arcana. But, while he often told us stories of the sea and of animals, he did not talk "shop" to us, as many people seemed to expect by their inquiries whether we did not receive quite a scientific education from his companionship.

At the same time, he was anything but a Bohemian. His inborn gaiety and high spirits, his humour and love of adventure, found from the first a balance in his love of science; and the rough experience of his early days intensified by contrast the spiritual serenity of united love. Lack of order, whether in mind or in outward surroundings, was no recommendation to him; and so far as the conventions represented in brief some valid results of social experience, he observed them and upheld them. They are not always dry husks out of which reason has evaporated. But where such were merely unreasoned custom, he was ready to set aside his mere likes and dislikes on good cause shown, and to follow reason as against the simple prejudice of custom, even his own.

On the whole, he made his impression on his children more by example than by spoken precept; much of his attitude may be gathered from a letter to his son on his twenty-first birthday :—

> You will have a son some day yourself, I suppose, and, if you do, I can wish you no greater satisfaction than to be able to say that he has reached manhood without having given a serious anxiety, and that you can look forward with entire confidence to his playing the man in the battle of life. I have tried to make you feel your responsibilities and act independently as early as possible; but, once for all, remember that I am not only your father but your nearest friend, ready to help you in all things reasonable, and perhaps in a few unreasonable.

After he had retired from his professorial work and settled down at Eastbourne, his grandchildren reaped the advantage of his leisure. His natural love for children had scope for expression, and children themselves had an instinctive confidence in the power and sympathy that irradiated his face and gave his square, rugged features the beauty of wisdom and kindliness. He could captivate them alike by lively fun and excellent nonsense, and by lucid explanations of the wonders of the world about which children love to hear. He fired one small granddaughter with a love of astronomy, and one day a visitor, entering unexpectedly, was startled to find the pair of them kneeling on the floor of the entrance hall before a large sheet of paper, on which the professor was drawing a diagram of the solar system, with a little pellet and a big ball to represent earth and sun, while the child was listening with rapt attention to an account of the planets and their movements, which he knew so well how to make simple and precise without ever being dull.

One of the most charming unions of the playful and serious was his letter to the small boy, still under five, who was reading *The Water Babies*, wherein his grandfather's name is genially made fun of among the authorities on Water Babies and Water Beasts of every description. Moreover, there is a picture by Linley Sambourne, showing Huxley and Owen examining a bottled Water Baby under big magnifying glasses. Now, as the child greatly desired more light on the reality of Water Babies, here was an authority to consult. And, as he had already learned to write, he indited a letter of inquiry, first anxiously asking his mother if he would receive in reply a "proper letter" that he could read for himself, or a "wrong letter" that must be read to him. The hint bore fruit, and to his carefully pencilled epistle :

> Have you seen a Water Baby? Did you put it in a bottle? Did it wonder if it could get out? Can I see it some day?

came a reply from his grandfather, neatly printed, letter

by letter, very unlike the orderly confusion with which
his pen usually rushed across the paper—to the great
perplexity, often, of his foreign correspondents and sometimes of correspondents nearer home :—

I never could make sure about that Water Baby.
I have seen Babies in water and Babies in bottles ;
but the Baby in the water was not in a bottle, and
the Baby in the bottle was not in water.

My friend who wrote the story of the Water
Baby was a very kind man and very clever.
Perhaps he thought I could see as much in the
water as he did. There are some people who see
a great deal and some who see very little in the
same things.

When you grow up I dare say you will be one of
the great-deal seers and see things more wonderful
than Water Babies where other folks can see
nothing.

There is a story of Mohammed that once, rather than
disturb a favourite cat, he cut off the sleeve of his robe on
which it lay asleep. Whether in like circumstances my
father would have done the same—had flowing sleeves
been a Victorian fashion—I cannot certainly say, though
he once was found similarly dispossessed of his favourite
study chair ; but he always regarded this anecdote as
displaying an agreeable trait in the Prophet. For he
himself was very fond of animals, and, though we seldom
kept dogs in London, cats were invariable members of the
household. Apropos of these, a letter may be quoted
which was written in 1893 in reply to an inquiry from a
journalist who was collecting anecdotes for an article on
the Home Pets of Celebrities :—

A long series of cats has reigned over my household for the last forty years, or thereabouts, but I
am sorry to say that I have no pictorial or other
record of their physical and moral excellences.

The present occupant of the throne is a large,

young, grey Tabby—Oliver by name. Not that he is in any sense a protector, for I doubt whether he has the heart to kill a mouse. However, I saw him catch and eat the first butterfly of the season, and trust that this germ of courage, thus manifested, may develop with age into efficient mousing.

As to sagacity, I should say that his judgment respecting the warmest place and the softest cushion in a room is infallible ; his punctuality at meal-times is admirable ; and his pertinacity in jumping on people's shoulders, till they give him some of the best of what is going, indicates great firmness.

XVIII

SOME LETTERS AND TABLE TALK

MY father's letters were seldom without a dash of
playfulness or humour somewhere; a thing always fresh
and spontaneous, unlike the calculated or laboured playfulness sometimes to be observed in the epistolary touch
of literary folk. A capital example is a note to Matthew
Arnold, at whose house he had left his umbrella. Arnold,
it may be added, had recently been critically engaged
upon the works of Bishop Wilson :—

> Look at Bishop Wilson on the sin of covetousness,
> and then inspect your umbrella stand. You will
> there see a beautiful brown smooth-handled umbrella
> which is *not* your property.
> Think of what the excellent prelate would have
> advised, and bring it with you next time you come
> to the Club. The porter will take care of it for me.

Sometimes the words will come trippingly from the
pen as if they were flung out in a brilliant flash of talk,
like the following sketch of human character :—

> Men, my dear, are very queer animals, a mixture
> of horse-nervousness, ass-stubbornness, and camel-
> malice—with an angel bobbing about unexpectedly
> like the apple in the posset—and when they can do
> exactly as they please they are very hard to drive.

As to his conversation, that, wrote the late Wilfrid
Ward,

> was singularly finished and (if I may so express it)
> clean cut; never long-winded or prosy; enlivened
> by vivid illustrations. He was an excellent *racon-
> teur*, and his stories had a stamp of their own

117

which would have made them always and every-
where acceptable. His sense of humour and
economy of words would have made it impossible,
had he lived to ninety, that they should ever have
been disparaged as symptoms of what has been
called " anecdotage."

Some fragments of his talk have been preserved by the
same hand. Speaking of Tennyson's conversation, he
said : " Doric beauty is its characteristic—perfect simplicity, without any ornament or anything artificial."

Telling how he had been to a meeting of the British
Museum Trustees, he said : " After the meeting Archbishop Benson helped me on with my greatcoat. I was
quite overcome by this species of spiritual investiture.
' Thank you, Archbishop,' I said ; ' I feel as if I were
receiving the pallium.' "

On another occasion he drew a distinction between
two writers, with neither of whom he sympathized.
" Don't mistake me. One is a thinker and man of
letters, the other is only a literary man. Erasmus was
a man of letters ; Gigadibs a literary man. A. B. is the
incarnation of Gigadibs. I should call him *Gigadibsius
Optimus Maximus*."

Of his quickness in rising to the occasion Professor
Howes tells a story. Staying after a lecture to answer
questions, he turned to a student and said : " Well,
I hope you understood it all." " All, sir, but one part,
during which you stood between me and the blackboard,"
was the reply ; the rejoinder : " I did my best to make
myself clear, but could not render myself transparent."

From among my own recollections I give the following :—" It is one of the most saddening things that, try
as we may, we can never be certain of making people
happy, whereas we can almost always be certain of
making them unhappy." Of the attitude towards

Spiritualism of a certain member of the Society for Psychical Research :—" He doesn't believe in it, yet lends it the cover of his name. He is one of those people who talk of the ' possibility ' of the thing, who think the difficulties of disproving a thing as good as direct evidence in its favour."

Again :—" It is very strange how most men will do anything to evade responsibility." Later, we were talking of the contrast between Hellene and Hebrew. " The real chosen people," he said, " were the Greeks. One of the most remarkable things about them is not only the smallness but the late rise of Attica, whereas Magna Graecia flourished in the eighth century. The Greeks were doing everything—piracy, trade, fighting, expelling the Persians. Never was there so large a number of self-governing communities.

" They fell short of the Jews in morality. How curious is the tolerant attitude of Socrates, like a modern man of the world talking to a young fellow who runs after the girls. The Jew, however he fell short in other respects, set himself a certain standard in cleanliness of life, and would not fall below it. The more creditable to him, because these vices were the offspring of the Semitic races among whom the Jew lived.

" There is a curious similarity between the position of the Jew in ancient times and what it is now. They were procurers and usurers among the Gentiles, yet many of them were singularly high-minded and pure. All, too, with an intense clannishness, the secret of their success, and a sense of superiority to the Gentile which would prevent the meanest Jew from sitting at table with a pro-consul.

" The most remarkable achievement of the Jew was to impose on Europe for eighteen centuries his own super-stitions—his ideas of the supernatural. Jahveh was no

more than Zeus or Milcom ; yet the Jew got established
the belief in the inspiration of his Bible and his law.   If
I were a Jew, I should have the same contempt as he
has for the Christian who acted in this way towards
me, who took my ideas and scorned me for clinging to
them."

Here may be quoted a passage from a letter to
Professor George Romanes :—

> I have a great respect for the Nazarenism of
> Jesus—very little for later "Christianity."   But
> the only religion that appeals to me is prophetic
> Judaism.   Add to it something from the best Stoics
> and something from Spinoza and something from
> Goethe, and there is a religion for men.   Some of
> these days I think I will make a cento out of the
> works of these people.

This cento, however, he never made.   Had he done so,
he would assuredly have illustrated his saying to Charles
Kingsley :—

> My business is to teach my aspirations to con-
> form themselves to fact ; not to try and make facts
> harmonize with my aspirations—

a notion expanded thus :—

> Science seems to me to teach in the highest and
> strongest manner the great truth which is embodied
> in the Christian conception of entire surrender to
> the will of God.   Sit down before fact as a little
> child, be prepared to give up every pre-conceived
> notion, follow humbly wherever and to whatever
> abysses nature leads, or you shall learn nothing.
> I have only begun to learn content and peace of
> mind since I resolved at all costs to do this.